BLACKJACK:
A WINNER'S HANDBOOK

Other books by Jerry Patterson

Blackjack's Winning Formula
Casino Gambling
Sports Betting
The Casino Gamblers' Winning Edge

BLACKJACK:
A WINNER'S HANDBOOK

Jerry L. Patterson

A Perigee Book

The reader should be advised that games of chance and sports betting are illegal in certain jurisdictions. The publisher and the author urge the reader before engaging in any gambling activity to determine the legality of any such game in his or her state.

Perigee Books
are published by
The Putnam Publishing Group
200 Madison Avenue
New York, NY 10016

Library of Congress Cataloging-in-Publication Data
Patterson, Jerry L.
Blackjack, a winner's handbook / Jerry L. Patterson.
p. cm.
Includes bibliographical references.
ISBN 0-399-51598-4 : price
1. Blackjack (Game) I. Title.
GV1295.B55P37 1990   90-7290 CIP
795.4'2—dc20

Cover design © by Bob Silverman
Cover photograph copyright © 1981 by Steve Kaplan

Printed in the United States of America
7 8 9 10

What the 1990's Edition of *Blackjack: A Winner's Handbook* Will Do for You

— Explain the changes in the game that occurred during the 1980s and show you how you can profit from them.

— Disclose that card counting does not always work and describe what you can do to avoid losing.

— Teach you how to play the game (if you are a beginning player) and show you a simple basic strategy for playing each and every blackjack hand to maximize your gain and minimize your loss.

— Describe one of the most powerful strategies ever devised—shuffle-tracking—and instruct you how to use it to control the game and give you a huge edge over the dealer.

— Expose those blackjack books, newsletters and courses that are still useful and those that are no longer viable in today's blackjack environment.

— Show you how to manage your gambling money so you're always in control, whether you're a beginner or advanced player.

— Provide a 5-step strategy for learning how to develop and use mental discipline to avoid losing and to increase your winning edge.

— Explain table biases caused by the casinos' non-random shuffle; how to avoid the dealer biases and how to turn the player biases to your advantage.

— Provide you with a 4-phased non-count strategy that minimizes losses while enabling you to score in those games where the dealer is breaking and the players are winning.

— Include strategies and tactics for card counters: new, innovative card-counting drills and three new, never-before-published winning strategies for the card counter to use in today's game.

— Tell you stories of team blackjack and teach you how to use team-play techniques to multiply your profits.

— Introduce a 7-step, winning program that will assist you to effectively utilize all of the powerful data in this book.

— Reveal extremely useful data for those blackjack players considering playing the game to make a living.

— Show you how to contact the author and join a network of blackjack winners!

About Jerry Patterson

BUSINESSMAN AND ENTREPRENEUR

Jerry enjoyed a successful twenty-five-year career in the computer-systems field which culminated as a part owner of a national computer-services firm. He is the proud owner and operator of the oldest and most successful casino gambling school in the country. *The Blackjack Clinic and School of Gambling* was established in 1978 and has graduated over 10,000 students. Jerry's winning methods, his honesty and integrity are the major reasons for this unparalleled success.

AUTHOR

Jerry is the author of five books in the casino gaming and sports field, all published by G. P. Putnam's Sons (the Perigee Division). Jerry has worked with the publisher to promote these books by appearing on scores of TV and radio shows. Feature articles about him have appeared in newspapers from New York City to Hong Kong.

PROFESSIONAL INVESTOR

Jerry has been a professional blackjack player, sports bettor and horse handicapper since the late 70s. He has been an investor in the stock market for over thirty years. He has been speculating in the options markets since they began operation in the early 70s.

SYNDICATED COLUMNIST

Jerry has written gaming columns for scores of newspapers around the country. A few examples are: *The Philadelphia Inquirer, The New York Daily News, The San Francisco Chronicle, The Los Angeles Herald-Examiner, The Atlantic City Press* and *The Orange County Register.*

CONSULTANT

During his twenty-five-year computer-systems career, Jerry served as a systems and management consultant to Fortune 500 corporations and to federal, state, regional and municipal governments. One of his greatest achievements was rebuilding the City of New Orleans' computer center, including hardware, software systems and staff retraining.

SYSTEM DEVELOPER

Jerry's penchant for research and data analysis has resulted in his developing many successful strategies for beating the casinos and the options markets. He holds the distinction of developing the first computer model to simulate the game of blackjack, and his *Stock Options Power Move Strategy* has made his clients a healthy return on their investment during the last bull market.

EDUCATIONAL BACKGROUND

BA From Willamette University in 1956
MS From George Washington University in 1968

To: The 100,000 + readers of the original edition of this book.
Your support convinced me, more than anything else,
of the necessity of doing this major update and rewrite.

Acknowledgments

Howard Schwartz of The Gambler's Book Club in Las Vegas for editing two crucial chapters.

Kathy Littel for explaining my shuffle-tracking methods, in chart form, much better than I ever could have.

Judy Linden, my editor at Putnam's, who graciously arranged for me the extra time needed to complete this book in its expanded and rewritten format. Judy performed an extremely creative job of editing the first version of the manuscript for this new edition. I am indebted to her for this because it really enhanced the readability and therefore the value of the book.

Contents

List of Charts

1

Introduction and Background

WHY THE 1990S EDITION OF *BLACKJACK: A WINNER'S HANDBOOK* WAS WRITTEN

The first edition of this book was self-published in 1977. The purpose was to assist the occasional gambler sift through the large amount of data on the game of casino blackjack, to avoid the worthless data and to ferret out those books and systems that would work well in a casino environment.

Resorts International Casino in Atlantic City was still six months away from opening when my wife, Nancy, began distributing the book in the fall of 1977. Because of the huge numbers of new gamblers flocking into Resorts and the awakening interest in casino gambling all over the East Coast, the book was an immediate success.

But the huge masses of gamblers fighting to get to the tables at Resorts and then The Boardwalk Regency (now Caesars), engendered the marketing of a plethora of blackjack books, systems, schools and learning aids, many of which were worthless.

Because of this deluge of blackjack data, we soon realized that my book was out-of-date and that an update was seriously needed. Nancy, having sold over 20,000 copies by this time, exhibited the book at the American Booksellers Association convention in Atlanta in 1979 and shopped the republication rights to several major New York publishing houses.

I wanted to go with Lyle Stuart's publishing house because of my common interest with Lyle in all the gambling games, but Nancy's choice prevailed and we sold the rights to the Perigee Division of The Putnam Publishing Group. This turned out to be an excellent decision because the revised and expanded edition, published in 1980, was distributed to almost every bookstore in the country and has now sold well over 100,000 copies. It has become the third-best-selling blackjack book of all time, behind only *Beat the Dealer* by Ed Thorp and *Playing Blackjack as a Business* by Lawrence Revere.

The game of casino blackjack changed dramatically during the 1980s, as you will soon learn. However, since I had neither the time nor the interest in doing a major rewrite, and since basic information was correct anyway, only minor revisions were incorporated in subsequent printings of the 1980s version.

However, in early 1989 it became apparent to both me and my publisher that *Blackjack: A Winner's Handbook* needed to be completely rewritten and revised.

The major reason is that changes in the game, introduced by the casinos, have made it much more difficult, in fact impossible in some casinos, to win by counting cards. This presents a problem for many neophyte gamblers because the books of the 1980s (my own included) give a far different opinion. It is necessary to bring to light the reasons why this has happened and, in so doing, help many occasional and serious gamblers avoid going down the wrong path.

I have instructed over 10,000 gamblers over the past twelve years, many of whom didn't contact me until they were quite a ways along in their study of card-counting systems and methodology. Some spent months studying complicated card-counting methods in their preparation to take on the casinos. Unfortunately, this time was wasted. Hopefully, the publication of this completely revised edition will steer its readers on the right track near the beginning of their blackjack-playing careers and avoid a lot of wasted time.

Don't get me wrong. You can still win by counting cards. But you have to be aware of the conditions under which winning is possible. And you have to understand that blackjack should not only be perceived as a game with a long-term advantage as it has traditionally, but also as a short-term game which we will redefine in this book.

There are non–card-counting strategies, such as hole-card play, developed in the late 1970s and 1980s, that are either obsolete or in the endangered species category. Some of these strategies worked well because certain conditions existed at that time. But these conditions no longer exist or are disappearing fast, and my purpose in this book is to call this to your attention and steer you clear of these losing tracks.

As mentioned previously, many of the blackjack books sold today are obsolete. Of course some are timeless and contain data that are as useful today as they were yesterday. Reading the wrong book can result in a tremendous amount of wasted time and lost money. I will list those books that belong in every blackjack player's library as well as those that should be avoided.

Most of the dozen or so blackjack newsletters that sprung up in the 1980s are out of business. But there are still four that publish newsletters dedicated exclusively to blackjack. Three of these are perpetuating, in my opinion, the myth that card counting still works for all blackjack games and under all blackjack conditions. There is one that recognizes the changes that have occurred and keeps you abreast of how to take advantage of them. All will be reviewed herein.

The primary purpose of this book is to teach you how to win in today's blackjack environment. Four winning strategies are published in this book; they are unique; you will not find them in any other book or newsletter. Three of these strategies involve card counting, but they recognize the advantages of playing table biases, which I will explain later in this book. These systems are complimented by detailed advice on bankroll management, learning drills for mastering the skills of card counting and an easy-to-use program for mental discipline.

Winning in today's blackjack environment requires that old skills and attitudes be changed and in some cases discarded. This book will assist you make these changes in your approach to becoming a winning player.

My field research with thousands of students and players has concluded that mental preparation is 90% of the game. If you are not mentally ready to play, no skill of any kind will work to help you win.

I am proud to announce that this book includes breakthrough data. A prominent Southern California psychologist, Dr. Steve Heller, founder and director of The Heller Institute, has given me permission to include some of his data on how to prepare mentally for a gambling trip and a gambling session. Steve has assisted me teach my blackjack classes for the past five years, and his tips presented herein have been used by hundreds of players to help them achieve success and to accomplish their blackjack goals.

When I teach in the classroom, I like to use case studies of successful players to illustrate various points. I am taking that same approach in this book. I have carefully screened the careers of several of my successful graduates and have chosen one to include in this book. It contains an excellent example of what I call the "Prime Success Factor." (This term will be defined in the case study.)

BLACKJACK: SHORT-TERM VS. LONG-TERM PERSPECTIVES

The casinos have a mathematical advantage in all the games of chance except blackjack. Blackjack can be approached as a game of skill. This skill, traditionally called card counting, gives the astute player a long-term advantage over the casino.

But how long is the long-term period of play? Players, mathematicians and computer scientists have been pondering this question for many years without coming up with a satisfactory answer.

To me, however, long-term play, or the long run, is longer than the average playing session or even the average trip of any casino gambler or blackjack player. For instance, most blackjack players visit Atlantic City for an evening, a day or a weekend. In Las Vegas a weekend is the usual duration. These playing-session durations have absolutely nothing to do with long-run mathematics.

In this book I will use the term "long run" to apply to traditional card counters, those players who are prepared to commit several hundred playing hours, under the proper playing conditions, to achieve a mathematical advantage over the casino.

But I will focus on the short-run, or short-term play, since this refers to the amount of time the majority of blackjack players devote to the game. The short run is what is happening right now, in this casino, at this blackjack table. In this book you will learn to recognize short-term opportunities and how to exploit them.

You will learn that playing a short-run strategy is different from playing a long-run strategy. For instance, if you have been playing blackjack for any length of time, you have learned traditional black-jack techniques that are accepted today as axioms such as basic strategy and card counting. This book takes a close look at these and other accepted blackjack traditions and departs from them for the benefit of the short-run player.

TRADITIONAL PLAYER VS. NEW-ERA PLAYER

There are two terms used in this book that relate to what has been said above: *traditional player* (or traditional card counter) and *new-era player*.

A *traditional player* is a person who uses a card-counting point-count system as his only winning tool and plays for the long run. He or she is not concerned with short-run fluctuations that may be due to table biases caused by the non-random shuffle. (These situations are described fully in later chapters.)

The term *new-era player* (also called "today's player") is used to define the player who understands that the game has changed and who is open to considering new winning strategies and tactics, other than card counting. The new-era player understands the advantages of recognizing and exploiting short-run opportunities.

It is my hope in writing this book that you will become a new-era player.

I also ask you to read this book with an open mind. If you are skeptical, set aside some time on your next casino visit for some observations. Select one or two ideas from this book and try to observe them in the real world of casino-played blackjack. You will find, without risking a dime, that they work!

OVERVIEW OF THE BOOK

The information in this book is presented in six parts.

Part I traces the evolution of blackjack systems and methods from the opening of Resorts International Casino in 1978 to the end of the 1980s. Six major developments are covered: Card counting in Chapter 2, Team Blackjack Play in Chapter 3, Shuffle-Tracking in Chapter 4, Concealed Computers in Chapter 5, Hole-Card Play in Chapter 6 and Biases Caused by the Non-Random Shuffle in Chapter 7. Chapter 8 concludes Part I with a Summary and Conclusions for Today's Player.

Since I was involved in all six of these developments and the changes engendered by them, I have written Part I in autobiographical form. I think you will find this quite interesting.

The purpose of Part I is to explain which of the many strategies connected with these six developments are obsolete and which strategies are still viable and yield profits if properly used.

Part II is a review and analysis of tools and techniques used to master play. Blackjack books are evaluated in Chapter 9 in four categories: (1) Top rated, (2) Contain some useful and practical information, (3) Of little or no use except to players wanting a complete library, (4) Not recommended. Other information such as schools, home-study courses and newsletters are evaluated in Chapter 10. Those that are still usable in today's environment are highlighted.

Part III presents winning strategies for both short-term and long-term blackjack players. "TAKEDOWN," the non-count strategy discussed in Chapter 13, exploits table biases and is unique to this book. It is based on my thirty-four years of blackjack play, blackjack research and blackjack instruction. It does not involve counting cards. It is a complete departure from accepted blackjack tradition because accepted blackjack tradition, such as card counting, does not always work in today's blackjack environment.

Chapter 11 leads off Part III with a primer on money management. An often overlooked part of most players' winning arsenal—mental discipline—is discussed in Chapter 12. Chapter 13 is TAKEDOWN—the 4-stage winning strategy for short-term players. Chapter 14 presents learning aids and drills for becoming a skilled card-counter, and Chapter 15 contains strategies and tactics for card counters. Chapter 16 puts it all together with a 7-step winning program for all players—long-term, short-term, card counter and non–card-counter.

One of the most-often-asked questions from blackjack players is covered in Part IV—How to Become a Professional Blackjack Player. Chapter 17 discusses fantasy and fact by delineating "Considerations for Turning Pro." Chapter 18 is an actual "Case Study of a Successful Pro" from the time the decision was made, to the accomplishment of the objective. One of the goals of most professional players is to travel the world, live a life of luxury, turn fantasy into reality and pay for all of it with blackjack winnings. One such exciting trip is selected from Jerry Patterson's blackjack diary to give meaning to this goal: a blackjack trip to Macao (a Portuguese colony near Hong Kong), which is described in Chapter 19.

Part V is for people who are beginning blackjack players and don't yet completely understand the rudiments of the game. Simple explanations of the rules of play are presented in Chapter 20 and a glossary of terms is included as Chapter 21. Beginning players should read Part V first and then come back to Part I.

Part VI, Chapter 22, lists sources of blackjack information including gambling-related bookstores, Jerry Patterson's Blackjack Network and instructional programs offered by Jerry Patterson.

A reader response card and information request card is included in the back of the book. If you have questions about any aspect of this book or wish further information about my instructional programs, please feel free to contact me.

Your learning curve will advance rapidly as a result of reading this book. If you follow the principles documented herein, you will indeed be able to do what few gamblers do—take the casinos' money instead of giving yours to them.

PART ONE

Evolution of Blackjack Systems and Methods in the 1980s

2

Card-Counting Pros and Cons

HOW IT ALL BEGAN: PUBLIC INTEREST IN BLACKJACK

May 28, 1978: Resorts International Casino opens in Atlantic City.

Eight months after the gambling referendum passed it finally happens—gambling in a state other than Nevada; the first gambling casino opens in Atlantic City.

Resorts is a mob scene. Television cameras and reporters are everywhere—in the hotel and on the casino floor (one of the few times, by the way, that cameras are allowed on the casino floor). The casino is so crowded that you can hardly move. Don't even think about getting to a blackjack table. Those players lucky enough to get in the door are lined up three deep behind every table, waiting to lose their money. Lines outside the casino, controlled by beefy security guards, snake along the Boardwalk waiting their turn to take a shot at the tables or the slots. Most of them don't get in on this opening day.

I use my "press credentials" from *The Philadelphia Inquirer*, the newspaper that is publishing my gambling column, to get involved in this opening-day scene. I get to the casino two hours early and enjoy mingling with the thousands of early-bird gamblers who want to be part of history—the first to lose their money at Resorts Casino.

Ten A.M. The casino opens. All of us rush to get a seat. I end up at a $5 table and settle in for the day. There is no chance of changing tables because of the mob waiting for each and every seat at each and every table.

There are two very significant points to make about this opening-day scene.

The first point is that, unlike Las Vegas, the gambling public was residing close to the scene. Eighty million people live within a day's drive of Atlantic City. The gambling public has easy access to Resorts Casino. A gambler could drive in for a two-hour session in the evening or a day's play on the weekend.

Secondly, because Resorts Casino was situated so close to its marketplace, this scene would be repeated many, many times over the next few months and up until the time when the second casino opened in Atlantic City almost a year later. If you wanted a seat at a blackjack table in Resorts Casino, you had to get in line at 8 A.M. or earlier—two hours before the casino opened at 10 A.M. If you were a $2 bettor, you had to know the general location of the $2 tables because these were always the ones to fill up first.

More and more gamblers began to focus on the blackjack game. With so many blackjack books on the market explaining that card counting could be used to get an edge over the house, and with my column in *The Philadelphia Inquirer* and my blackjack clinics educating the gambling public, many soon realized there was something special about this game.

Public interest was intensified because of the "early-surrender decision" explained in my column in the *Inquirer* a couple of months after Resorts opened. The blackjack surrender decision means that if you don't like the first two cards dealt to you, you simply "surrender" them back to the dealer, giving up half your bet. Early surrender means that, when the dealer shows a 10-value card or ace, a potential blackjack, you may surrender early or before the dealer ascertains whether or not he or she has the blackjack. Julian Braun, of the IBM Corporation, determined that, employing the early-surrender decision with his mathematically derived basic strategy, the player actually had a small edge over the house: 0.25%! (This means that out of each $100 bet, the player wins 25 cents; not too much, but the important point is that it is a positive advantage.)

The significance of the early-surrender decision will be discussed in the chapter on team blackjack.

A BRIEF LESSON ON CARD COUNTING

Since there is a long history behind the tradition of card counting and its recognition as a valid strategy, I feel I should give you some information about how to count. Once you understand the concept, you can understand the problems with card counting which will be discussed next.

Counting does not take a good memory, because there is nothing to memorize. All you have to understand is that there are high cards, low cards and neutral cards in a 52-card deck. In fact, there is an equal number of high and low cards.

In the standard High-Low Point-Count System, low cards are 2 through 6; high cards are 10s, picture cards and aces; neutral cards are 7s, 8s, and 9s.

Here are the values of these three categories of cards:

2 through 6 = +1; 10s, pictures and aces = −1; 7s, 8s and 9s = 0

Starting with zero off the top of a deck of cards or dealing shoe, all you do is add + 1 for each low card you see dealt, subtract a 1 for every high card you see dealt, and repeat the count so you won't forget it when you see a neutral card or 0.

As the count goes up, it means there are more low cards being dealt (they have a "plus" value) and more high cards, left in the shoe, remaining to be dealt. If the count is minus, it means that there are more low cards in the shoe remaining to be dealt.

Since a shoe rich in high cards favors the player (for example, a better chance of drawing a blackjack) and a shoe rich in low cards favors the dealer (who will therefore break less often and win more hands), the count gives the player a mathematical assessment of his or her chances of winning the next hand. If his chances are good, the bet is increased. If they are poor, the player makes a minimum bet.

The plus count is a consequence of more low cards being dealt than high cards, and since there is an equal number of each in the deck, a plus count means that there are more 10s and aces remaining in the deck to be played than low cards. This creates the possibilities of more player blackjacks with the payoff of 1.5 to 1 (the dealer gets no such payoff on his blackjacks), more dealer breaking on stiff hands (hands totaling 12 through 16; rules of play stipulate that the dealer must hit his hand until it totals 17 or more), and more double-down wins (the doubling of a bet on the first two cards) for the player (for example, drawing a 10-value card to an 11 for a hand totaling 21).

Essentially, the player is betting more when he has the advantage, and less when the dealer has the advantage. Therefore a profit is realized over the long run.

The count can also be used to play the hand, but this tactic is beyond the scope of this brief lesson and will be taken up in Chapter 14.

CARD-COUNTING SYSTEMS

With the increasing popularity of the game following the opening of the Atlantic City casinos, research projects multiplied. Much of this research was done by college professors who rarely, if ever, saw the inside of a casino. And some was performed by blackjack players with statistical skills who enjoyed figuring out a basic strategy play to the third decimal place (a neat academic exercise but hardly useful inside a casino).

The initial thrust focused on the development of point-count systems that determined the optimum values to assign the various cards to maximize the players' theoretical advantage. Arguments went on among these researchers for years as to the merits of the various levels of point-count systems and about the values of the points assigned to each card. For example, a Level I system would assign the numbers 1, -1 and 0 to the card types while a Level II system would assign 1, -1, 2, -2 and 0. Level IV was the highest of the levels with values from $+4$ to -4.

My recommendation to you in the original edition of this book still stands: If you haven't learned to count, learn the High-Low Point-Count System described earlier in this chapter. If you have learned a Level I count with the ace valued as −1, do not change; your count will work just as well as High-Low. If you have learned a single-level count with the ace valued as zero, change your point-count assignments to agree with High-Low: 2-6 = +1;7,8,9 = 0; 10s, face cards and aces = −1.

If you have learned a multiple-level count, I recommend that you discard it and learn High-Low.

Here are two reasons why:

1. Many advanced, multiple-level count systems count the ace as zero. The ace is the most important card in the deck. If it's assigned a value of zero, it has a neutral value. Therefore, to achieve maximum effectiveness from your point-count system, you must keep a side count of aces and factor this side count into your betting and playing decisions. Even professional blackjack players have difficulty with this practice. Recreational players who try it are prone to error.

That leaves us with two choices for the ace: assign it a value of + 1 and call it a small card. Or assign it a value of −1 and call it a high card. There was a system published in the early days of card counting called the "One/two Count" that valued 10s at −2 and all others, including the ace, as +1. It was an attempt to transform Thorp's Ten Count System (as published in his book *Beat the Dealer*—reviewed in Chapter 9) to a Point-Count System. It did not work except in a single-deck game. Research and computer studies showed that the level of betting and playing effectiveness was sharply reduced when this system was employed.

The best approach is to define the ace as a high card and assign it a value of −1.

2. If you are considering learning an advanced point-count system such as the Revere APC or the Uston APC, here are my comments based on conversations with hundreds of blackjack players and my own thirty-five years of casino blackjack experience. Don't do it. First of all, it will take you hundreds of hours to practice and perfect all the nuances for using the count to bet and play the hands. Secondly, the small additional paper advantage you gain will quickly evaporate in the real world of casino play. I have talked to players

who have spent months practicing an advanced point-count system only to go to the casino and crumble under the pressure of making split-second decisions. When they call me for advice it is difficult to tell them they have wasted their time, but this is what I have to do. Many of those who followed my advice have gone on to become consistent winning players.

WHY THE COUNT DOES NOT ALWAYS WORK

The evolution of blackjack systems and methods in the 1980s unfolded along two major research pathways: Pathway 1—changes to card-counting systems and methods; and Pathway 2—changes engendered by the recognition of the non-random shuffle and its impact on the *application of systems and methods in the real world of casino play.* I was involved in both of these pathways and the major cause of the diversion of Pathway 2. I will now discuss how this diversion came about and how it rendered many strategies in Pathway 1 ineffective. It is important for you to understand this diversion to Pathway 2 now so you can better understand the new strategies presented later. First, however, some background:

My recognition that card counting doesn't always work did not happen overnight. It started with two incidents. The first was a chance conversation I had with a blackjack player in a business-supply store about seven years ago. I had stopped in to pick up some office supplies, and the proprietor, knowing me as a blackjack instructor and knowing the other fellow as a player, naturally introduced us. We got to talking and this guy told me that I had the game figured out all wrong.

"Why bet up when the count is rising?" he said. "This is when the low cards are coming out and the dealer has the advantage."

"But there are more high cards left in the shoe and you have a better chance of getting one," I countered. "Everybody knows that more high cards left in the shoe gives the player a greater chance of winning—he will be dealt more blackjacks, win more double downs and the dealer will break more often on stiff hands."

"You've got it backwards," he said. "I bet up when the count is minus and when more high cards are coming out."

I dismissed this guy as a nut, left the store and forgot all about it—until about ten days later when I was in the Golden Nugget (now Bally's Grand) and playing in a $25 game. This is when the second incident occurred.

About one deck had been dealt in this 6-deck game when the count began to move up very rapidly. (Note to novice players: when the count moves up, it means that more low cards, counted as +1, are being dealt; the player has a mathematical advantage because the remaining shoe is rich in 10s, face cards and aces.) My bet began to move up with the count. I lost a $50 bet. The count continued to move higher. I lost a $100 bet. By this time 3 decks have been dealt and the count is +15. The True Count is now +5 (True Count = running count of +15 divided by 3 decks remaining. The True Count is a mathematical reflection of the odds of winning the next hand). I bet the True Count in my $50 units (a $250 bet). I lost. The count is now +20. I bet $300. I double down with an 11 and draw a 3. The dealer shows a 7, turns over an 8 and I feel a surge of adrenaline with this reprieve. Surely, with over 20 extra high-cards left in this shoe, the dealer will draw one and break. No such luck. He draws a 2 for a 17. I'm out another $600. The count is now +24 and there are just over 2 decks left to play before the shuffle. A "True" of around 12 gives me about a 6% advantage on the next hand. I bet $500. By this time a crowd has gathered around the table, two of whom are my students who have stopped to watch the Master play. What they saw was the Master lose another hand.

This shoe got me to thinking about that conversation ten days ago. If my "friend" from the office-supply company had been in this game he would have said: "I told you so." What had happened, as I was later to learn, is that *I played into a clump of low cards.* The extra high cards that my count indicated were in the shoe were never dealt. They were behind the cut card. Without knowing it, I was playing into a devastating dealer advantage!

"So what!" you may be asking, especially if you are an experienced card counter. Anything can happen in a blackjack game. The next time you find yourself in a hot shoe you could win all that back and then some.

This line of thinking is indeed correct. But, nevertheless, these two incidents led me into a research project the outcome of which totally changed my thinking about the game of blackjack. I learned why the count does not always work.

Consider the case when you are losing on a high count. The reason is this: The count keeps going up because low cards are being dealt. Low cards favor the dealer and you are playing in the midst of a low-card clump. This clump of low cards is a *dealer bias*.

Now consider the case when you are winning on a low count. The count is minus because high cards are being dealt. You are playing in the midst of a high-card clump and winning. This is called a *player bias*.

Things are working out just the opposite of the way they are supposed to, aren't they? Granted, it doesn't always happen this way; in a shoe with well-shuffled cards, the high cards will come out when the count goes up. But in a game with like-card clumping, betting with the count can be devastating because the high cards just don't come out, as low card after low card is dealt and the dealer doesn't break.

These clumps are caused by the *non-random shuffle*. Insufficient shuffling of eight, six, four or even a single deck of cards produces favorable or unfavorable clumps than can last from one shoe to the next.

It is very important that you understand fully why card counting doesn't always work. Let's continue this discussion by posing some questions.

QUESTIONS FOR A TRADITIONAL CARD COUNTER

How many times have you sat at a table in a minus-count situation, making minimum bets and winning hand after hand when, according to card-counting theory, you "should have been" losing? When you left the table with a smaller profit than most of the other "unskilled players," did you question the value of the count since it did not alert you to a winning situation? How much more could you have made if you had raised your bets as the other players at the table did?

How many times have you lost hand after hand in a high count with your maximum bet out? There is no greater frustration than betting up when the count skyrockets only to be beaten by the dealer hand after hand after hand.

Have you ever been the only losing player at a table with a high count? Everyone else kept getting the high cards and you kept getting the poor hands?

Has there ever been a time when you lost a lot of money playing heads-up (just you and the dealer)? When you walked away from the table, did it ever occur to you that the reason no one was playing against that dealer was because the dealer was "hot" and had sent the players scurrying away with their losses?

The reason all these situations develop is because in the real world of casino blackjack, there is such a thing as a biased game. And there is nothing you can do to change the bias since the cards are already situated. In the real world of casinos and dealers . . .

Card counting is no longer enough!

I have been showing you in this chapter why card counters have a mathematical edge over the casinos. And I have posed a very important question: Why does the high count sometimes not work at all, and why does the low count (when you are supposed to lose) sometimes produce winning hands?

Here is a general answer to the question: Some games have a bias in favor of the dealer and some games have a bias in favor of the player.

To give you a specific answer, let me introduce you to the notion of blackjack biases by explaining what I mean by biases and how they affect the count.

AN INTRODUCTION TO BIASES CAUSED BY THE NON-RANDOM SHUFFLE

Most blackjack books state that card counting has been tested in the computers and that you will win about 1.5% of all the money you bet if you count cards correctly and bet correctly according to the count.

That is very true *if you are playing within the confines of a computer.* In a computer, the cards are never shuffled. There *are* no cards—only random numbers generated by a computer program. The computer program spits out numbers randomly. Random means that, theoretically, each number has exactly the same chance of coming up as any other.

In a major study conducted by Dr. Persi Diaconis, of Harvard University, and Dr. Dave Bayer, a mathematician and computer scientist at Columbia University, it was proved that 7 shuffles are necessary to randomly mix a single deck of cards, and that 12 shuffles are necessary to randomly mix six decks of cards (the number of decks found in most shoe games).

In the casino, there is no such thing as randomly shuffled cards. The dealer shuffles between three and five times before dealing a new round in a single-deck game, and once or twice only in a shoe game. The casino's objective is to keep the game going, take your money as quickly as possible, and make room for the next player, who they hope will be another loser. More time spent on the shuffle means more down time, with no bets being made. This costs the casinos money.

The type of shuffle employed and the number of times the decks are shuffled is a business decision usually made at the casino-manager level. And this decision is usually made to maximize the casino's bottom line.

Comparing the computer-played game of blackjack with random numbers to the real game of blackjack with its non-random shuffle is like comparing apples to oranges. Until I realized this, I thought everything was accurate in the card-counting research. In my earlier books, I recommended the High-Low Point Count. I still feel that particular count is the best one for professional players. It is simple and easier to use than a multi-level count. That's why we teach it.

But players who understand biases have an advantage over traditional players who use the count only. They can select tables where the count works well because of these biases. When they find a table that has a bias in their favor, the count works better than ever. In

Chapter 7 you will learn how to recognize a bias and about a strategy called TARGET 21 for detecting and exploiting biases.

Card counting and card-counting research projects had a major influence on the evolution of blackjack systems and methods in the 1980s. For example, another major research thrust involved optimal bet sizing with the Kelly Criterion. The Kelly Criterion, simply stated, means that your bet size should be related to your mathematical advantage on the next hand to be played. Computer simulations and complex mathematical formulas were used to determine these bet sizes according to bankroll size and relate them to the True Count, which is a mathematical reflection of the player's odds of winning the next hand.

I participated in a number of these projects and enjoyed them immensely. I used the results of this research to teach an Advanced Card-Counting Clinic and to establish betting guidelines for my blackjack teams.

But I learned something about the Kelly Criterion in the two to three years that I used it: It does not take into account the realities of the cards coming out of a shoe in a real blackjack game. It works well in a computer environment, and it works well in a game with the cards and the count going my way, i.e., "I am winning." But, if I have lost three hands in succession, the dealer is getting the high cards on the high count, and the count keeps going up, Kelly doesn't consider what has happened in these last three hands. Kelly tells me to make an even bigger bet on the next hand. Kelly is jeopardizing my bankroll!

I have mentioned that there were two major research and development pathways in the 1980s: the card-counting pathway (Pathway 1) and the pathway concerned with player biases engendered by the non-random shuffle (Pathway 2).

In our discussion of the evolution of blackjack systems and methods in the 1980s, we will review interesting projects on the development of winning blackjack systems from both of these pathways. In your development as a winning blackjack player, it is important that you understand "where we came from" so that you can fully appreciate "where we are going."

One of the most fascinating and effective of all Pathway 1 methods is team blackjack. Let's get into it!

3

Team Play

THE ATLANTIC CITY "CANDY STORE"

When Resorts International Casino opened in May of 1978, little
did anyone realize at the time the impact this event would have on
the development of winning systems to beat the game of casino
blackjack. This was because the rules of the game were the most
favorable in the world and not only benefited occasional players but
also encouraged skilled and professional players to flock to Atlantic
City.

Here is what happened.

In an attempt to give the gaming public a favorable game, the
gaming commissioners of the State of New Jersey approved four
rules that created what professional blackjack players refer to as a
"candy store." These rules existed between May 1978 and September 1981. The first rule was "surrender."

Surrender means giving up your hand after the first two cards are
dealt. Your chances of beating the dealer are slim, so you announce
the decision orally: "I surrender." The dealer picks up your hand and
takes half your bet. The difference between the surrender decision
and the early-surrender decision involves the dealer's hole card and
whether or not the dealer has blackjack. You are not allowed to
surrender against a dealer blackjack; in other words you must lose
your entire bet; you cannot surrender and save half of it. But you
can early surrender against a blackjack. This is what the "early"

means: you surrender "early," before the dealer checks the hole card to determine whether or not he has blackjack. According to the mathematics of blackjack, this rule subtracts only about $\frac{1}{10}$th of 1% from the house advantage over the basic-strategy player. However, if you couple surrender with the second rule change, early surrender, you have the most favorable player decision in blackjack. This occurred because the second rule prohibited the dealer from checking the hole card (the dealer is dealt one card up and one card down, the down card is called the hole card) until after all the players had played their hands.

To better understand the impact of these two rules, visualize the following hand. You are dealt a 10, 6 against a dealer's ace up-card. Your chances of winning are very, very small. If you hit the 16, you will most likely break. If you stand, the dealer, with an ace, will probably make his or her hand. With an ace showing, the dealer breaks only about 12% of the time. But, betting $10 on the hand, you employ the early-surrender rule. The dealer scoops up your cards and takes half of your bet, or $5.

When the dealer's turn comes, he turns over a king for a blackjack. Do you see the advantage? You have only lost half your bet against a blackjack!

Blackjack's mathematicians quickly worked out a playing strategy for this very favorable rule, and guess what? Using a mathematically derived strategy for playing the hands, the player now held an advantage over the house! A small but very significant 0.25%. The tables had turned.

There's yet a third rule without which the Atlantic City Candy Store would not have opened for business. The dealer was required to deal two-thirds of a shoe before shuffling. Now if you understand card counting, you'll understand how easy it was to win while this Candy Store was open. When the remaining deck to be played— that is, those cards left in the shoe—is rich in 10s and aces, the player has an advantage on the next hand. The size of that advantage is determined by the number of extra 10-value cards and aces—the more the better. The player had it all his own way; the third rule prohibited the dealer from shuffling up when the card counter raised his bet on hands on which he held the advantage. For example, if the count determined that the dealer had the advantage on the next hand, the counter might bet $5. But if the counter held the advantage on the next hand he might bet $100 or more.

Put these three rules together with a fourth rule that said the casinos were not allowed to bar blackjack players from play, and you have the most favorable blackjack game ever offered in this country. For instance, if you raise your bet from $5 to $100 in Nevada, the pit boss comes over and announces "that's your last hand" and politely shows you to the door. But not so in Atlantic City. You could raise your bet to table maximum if your bankroll permitted it, and they couldn't do anything but grit their teeth and watch you rake the chips off the table. (This no-barring rule was reversed in early 1979.)

This game was made to order for blackjack teams, and they began invading Atlantic City in earnest in December of 1979.

At the time Team Play was the most powerful and most feared of all of blackjack's winning weapons. It is still a usable technique today, and I will show you how after explaining what it is and how it works.

HOW TEAM PLAY WORKS

Consider the following scenario:

You are a card counter sitting at a blackjack table, patiently counting down the deck and waiting for a favorable situation to develop. But let's assume the high cards and aces are played early in the shoe and you never get that favorable situation during the entire shoe. You've spent a lot of wasted time.

But now let's change the scenario. You are a big player with a team of counters deployed throughout the casino. One of your counters gives you a signal to enter the game and then signals a very high count. The pit bosses don't know what's going on because no words are spoken—it's all done with hand signals. You enter the game and immediately make a big bet. You stay until the count goes down and the game turns unfavorable. You then depart and wait to be called in to another favorable game by another of your counters. You have a tremendous advantage because your time is optimized, you are betting big only on high-count favorable situations, and you are playing with a joint bankroll that all members of the team kick into.

For example, suppose you had ten blackjack players, all playing with a $5000 bankroll. Now they form a team, pool their money and play to a $50,000 bankroll. Accepted money-management theory says that a counter should not bet more than 2% of his or her total bankroll. **Two percent of $50,000, or $1000, is a lot more than 2% of $5000, or just $100.** This is called leverage and it is the major advantage of Team Play.

It took the Nevada casinos awhile to catch on, and when they did, they instituted countermeasures and barred all suspected counters from play, including a man named Kenny Uston and his teams.

Kenny Uston, God rest his soul, learned this technique from Al and perfected it to an extremely high degree of profitability. Kenny and his teams had been working Nevada until Resorts opened; then they "took over" the Candy Store in December 1978.

Ed Thorp, in the first edition of his book *Beat the Dealer*, conceived the idea of Team Play. This was back in 1961. It's amazing that the idea was not implemented until the mid-70s, some fifteen years later.

But Kenny and his teams made up for lost time. They took millions off the tables during the mid- to late-70s before they were barred from most Nevada casinos.

I'll never forget the first time I met Kenny. He was playing blackjack at Resorts in Atlantic City in December of 1978. I recognized him by the familiar curly hair and beard. Betting stacks of green, he was losing heavily. "You don't want any part of this holocaust," he said to a friend. My wife, Nancy, much more assertive than I, arranged for me to meet Kenny and we enjoyed a pleasant dinner together at the Knife and Fork restaurant. Kenny invited me to play on his blackjack team, just forming at the time. I admit I was dazzled by the status, glamour and the prospects of quick money. But I turned him down, preferring instead to maintain a longer blackjack career. Kenny burned out team members very quickly. Once you become known to the casinos, it is difficult to make money playing blackjack.

But I took what I learned from Kenny and formed a number of

my own blackjack teams. The heyday of the blackjack teams was during 1979 and 1980, and I was right in the middle of it. I organized, managed and played on five blackjack teams during this period.

Team Play has advantages and disadvantages. I've told you about the major advantages of leverage and time optimization. But there is a disadvantage you must understand before you can use the tips on Team Play that will conclude this chapter. I will use some personal experiences to make my point.

JERRY PATTERSON'S BLACKJACK TEAMS

I formed Team 1 with my blackjack instructor Bob, a person I personally trained to teach all the Blackjack Clinics I was conducting at the time. The team consisted of just the two of us, and we each ponied up $3750 to form a joint bank of $7500. Sometimes we played together and sometimes we played apart, but we trusted each other implicitly. We were not using Kenny's "Big Player" approach (one player making big bets when called into tables by a team of counters), preferring instead to take advantage of the leverage of the joint bank. It took us a little over fifty hours of play to double this bank.

We then formed Team 2 and added a third partner, Bill, an outstanding player who was a commodities broker. Bill had graduated from one of my Clinics and just loved to play blackjack. We each antied up $5000, so our joint bank was $15,000. Our approach was the same. We played together and separate, but we all played as though the full $15,000 were behind us. In other words, our maximum bet was 2% of $15,000, or $300, instead of 2% of $5000, or just $100, so we were getting a leverage factor of 3 by playing as a team. It took us a little over one hundred playing hours to double this bank. A profit of about $150 per playing hour. Not too shabby!

Having doubled $15,000 to $30,000, we then formed Team 3 and took in a fourth partner. His name was Danny. Bob, Bill and I put up the full $30,000 and Danny added his talent and his time; he didn't have any money but he was an excellent card counter. By this time I had purchased two duplexes in Atlantic City. I rented one of them to the team and Danny moved in. He did not have a job, so he moved into the house and played full-time. Bill, Bob and I were working at the time. I had by this time sold out my interest in my computer company and formed my Blackjack Clinics instruction business, which was doing extremely well; we were instructing over one hundred students a month in classes running almost every day of the week.

Bob, Bill and I played as time permitted, usually three or four days a week. Since Danny was playing full-time, we funded his play with half the bank, or $15,000. In the beginning all went well as Danny quickly won over $10,000. And because of the big bucks he was betting and the time he was playing, the casino pit bosses were giving Danny anything he wanted—from gourmet meals to luxury suites.

Then the bank began to dwindle. It seemed that whatever the three of us won, Danny lost this and then some. So the total bank gradually decreased from around $42,000 at its high point to just $27,000. Since we started with $30,000, the bank suffered a total loss of $3000. This was for one month's time duration and over one hundred joint playing hours. This could have been just a statistical swing, but the three of us felt something was clearly wrong.

There was. Danny was skimming! He was keeping money won for himself and reporting only losses. He finally broke down and told us. He was in tears and very emotionally distraught. He claimed that he was upset because he was putting in all the hours and we weren't contributing our share of the playing time.

Team bankroll practice pays based on money invested, time played and money won, so Danny was certainly going to get his share based on his hours and his win. But the high life was just too much for him.

He begged us for another chance and we gave it to him based on my recommendation. We decided to let Danny go when the bank ground at the $27,000 level for the next three weeks. A $3000 loss and many, many playing hours of wasted time for Bob, Bill and myself. The three of us continued to play part-time for the next two months and eventually broke the bank when it reached $45,000—a $5000 profit for each of us but really not worth all the wasted time.

The major problem with Team Play is honesty. How do you know if a team member is reporting his or her wins and losses honestly?

Kenny used lie-detector tests for all his teams. And I did this for my Teams 4 and 5. But even if a polygraph gives you a favorable report, this is only at one point in time. What happens after the team is formed and money starts changing hands? On Kenny's teams, any member suspecting any other member of skimming could call for a polygraph at any time. But this became cumbersome and caused much distrust when it happened. I did not implement this policy on my Teams 4 and 5. Instead I trusted our judgment in the selection of team members and accepted a favorable polygraph report for confirmation.

On Team 4 I got burned again. Our joint $60,000 bank went nowhere for over two months and we learned that Jimmy, the team member with the best winning record, was skimming. One of the advantages of Team Play, given equal ability, is less risk: If one member is losing, one or more are probably winning, so team bankroll fluctuations are reduced. Jimmy was on a hot streak and could not lose. Other team members were not doing so well. Jimmy made himself believe that he was contributing more than his fair share because of his big wins. It therefore was OK for him to skim some off the top and not report the skimmed win. We immediately fired Jimmy and Team 4 performance improved dramatically.

I also implemented more stringent money-control procedures through the team manager. My manager kept complete control of the bankroll. He coordinated and was involved in every team blackjack playing session. He would release the session bankroll prior to the session, monitor each team member's performance during the session (all members played in the same casino), and collect the money, including money won if any, immediately after the session.

Money control became the accepted operational procedure, and from this point on I had no more problems with skimming.

Even with the problems of dishonesty, blackjack teams flourished in Atlantic City in the early '80s. At one point there were over six professional teams in operation, including one that I had trained in my Team Blackjack Clinic. One of these teams, from Czechoslovakia, was the first, to my knowledge, to use Shuffle-Tracking, a method discussed in the next chapter.

Team Play subsided considerably after September 1981, when the early-surrender decision was abolished and when the casinos were allowed to use an 8-deck shoe (an 8-deck shoe introduces more cards into the game, thereby reducing the number of favorable high-count betting opportunities and the players' advantage). Then another change instituted by the New Jersey Gaming Commission made Team Play even more difficult: The casinos were allowed to restrict a player's bet size to the table minimum if he or she entered in the middle of a shoe and was suspected by the pit boss of being a card counter. This decision effectively abolished Kenny Uston's Big Player Strategy.

Is Team Play still effective? Yes. Although I personally have made much more money playing alone than with a team, I recognize the advantages to playing as a team if the problems cited above can be eliminated, if money control is used, if a strong team manager is in charge and if appropriate casino conditions can be found.

And Team Play, contrary to popular opinion, does not have to involve playing with a joint bankroll. There are other advantages such as scouting for winning tables and sharing this information that can make team play very effective.

TIPS ON TEAM PLAY

As far as investment and finances are concerned, this is how a traditional blackjack team operates. A joint bankroll is formed from money invested by the players and perhaps non-players as well. The objective is to double the bank. When this objective is achieved, the profits are carved up as follows:

- 50% is divided up among the investors in proportion to how much each invested. For example, if one investor puts up half the bank, he or she gets half of this 50% piece of the bank.
- 25% is divided up among the players according to hours played. For example, if one player plays 10% of the total team hours played, he or she gets 10% of this slice of the profits.
- 25% is divided up among the players according to money won.

For example, if one player wins 40% of the total dollars won by the team, he or she gets 40% of this part of the profits.

Team-Play techniques can also involve cooperation. Cooperation in finding playable tables. When you visit a casino with friends, consider working together! If you are card counters, each of you can scout for and find tables that meet your criteria and the criteria described in this book. If one of you is playing in a favorable game, you can signal your friend to enter the game.

I ran a Blackjack Training Academy for a number of years in the early '80s. And my students were much more comfortable using this approach to Team Play rather than the other technique. I called it "cooperative card counting." The approach is still viable under today's blackjack conditions.

Three players in one casino can monitor playing conditions much easier than one player. Think back to the last time you visited a casino with friends. What did you do? Probably went in your own direction after entering the casino and found and played at your own selected tables. Then you met your friends later for dinner or a drink. Next time try cooperation. It's more fun and more effective!

The Nevada and Atlantic City casinos have curtailed, but not totally stopped, organized Team Play. But legalized casino gambling is expanding well beyond the boundaries of these two locations. Iowa and Illinois have approved riverboat gambling, and South Dakota has approved gambling in Deadwood. Many other midwest states including Indiana are considering legalizing gambling as this book goes to press. Legalized gambling can be found on Indian reservations in many parts of the country. Canada has legalized gambling in Calgary and Winnipeg, and blackjack is played in scores of foreign countries including most European countries and many countries in Asia.

Organized Team-Play techniques can be applied to these games if you are prepared to make the investment of time and funds.

Many of the blackjack teams operating in the early 1980s used Shuffle-Tracking—one of the most powerful strategies to emerge from Research Pathway 1. Let's start at the beginning . . .

4

Shuffle-Tracking

JUST WHAT IS SHUFFLE-TRACKING?

"Shuffle-Truck."

It was an early February morning in 1981 and I was practicing card-counting drills in my Blackjack Academy when I first heard this word mentioned. Startled, I looked up. My friend Dick walked in. His business was in the same office complex as my Academy, and one of his services was polygraph tests.

"Shuffle-Truck. Those are the only words I can mention," he went on. "I just polygraphed a blackjack team from Czechoslovakia. I can't tell you what the questions and answers were because that's confidential. But the words—Shuffle-Truck—might give you a clue and some ideas to look into."

I thanked him. We chatted awhile and then he left.

These two words—Shuffle-Truck—were to start me on a year-long project that involved system development, hundreds of hours of successful personal play with the resulting winning system, and then the formation of Team 5.

I recognized the words right away because I was familiar with the concept. *"Shuffle-truck"* was German for shuffle-track. The concept of remembering the locations of certain clumps of cards in the discard tray and then tracking them through the shuffle and cutting them into play (favorable clumps) or out of play (unfavorable clumps) had been mentioned in one of the many blackjack newsletters published at that time.

Up until now I hadn't thought too much about it. But this was different—a blackjack team using a shuffle-tracking technique. Now. In Atlantic City. I was missing out on something big and I had to find out what was going on.

I immediately initiated a dual course of action. I asked my wife and partner, Nancy, if she would find the team and set up a dinner meeting with the team leader. In the meantime I started experimenting with the idea by dealing decks of shoes and watching what happened to clumps of cards as they moved from the discard tray, through various types of shuffles, and back into play.

I began to see the possibilities in a few short hours and had many ideas to discuss with the team leader, Vladimir, whom I met a week later.

By that time we were also hearing rumors about the huge wins the Czech team was taking out of the Atlantic City casinos. We had an interesting dinner with Vladimir, but I didn't learn much. His English was not too proficient and he really did not want to tell me all that much anyway. I don't blame him. It was obvious by the general tone of the conversation that his team was hugely successful. Its members had escaped from behind the Iron Curtain by learning to play winning blackjack with this shuffle-tracking technique. They were playing and winning in casinos all over the world. Of course they had come to Atlantic City when they heard about the great rules.

Remember, at this time the casino pit bosses had no idea whatsoever of this devastating new method. It didn't look like card counting to them, because players would bet big right off the top of a new shoe. At that time it was virtually undetectable.

After this meeting I continued to practice and began to develop some ideas for how to track the clumps. A few more weeks and my system was ready for a casino test.

HOW SHUFFLE-TRACKING WORKS

I would keep a high-low count (aces and 10-value cards = −1; 2 through 6 = +1; 7,8,9 = 0) as the shoe was dealt out. At the

end of each deck I would mark the count, using the clock positions on a chip. For example, if the count was +9, meaning 9
more low cards had been played than high cards, I would turn the
face of the chip to the 9 o'clock position. Minus counts were han-
dled the same way, but with the chip moved off-center to signify
the minus. At the end of a 6-deck shoe with 4 decks dealt out, I
knew the content of each half-deck dealt—whether or not it was
rich in extra high cards (favorable to the player) or rich in low
cards (favorable to the dealer).

Now the dealer had to cooperate for the system to work. During
the shuffle if the dealer picked up one half-deck in each hand and
then shuffled the two half-decks together, I knew the content of that
deck. For example, assume that the dealer picked up a half-deck in
his left hand with 7 extra high cards and a half-deck in his right hand
with 6 extra high cards. He shuffled these together and placed the
resulting one-deck stack aside ready for the next shoe. I now knew
that this one-deck stack contained 13 extra high cards. This is very,
very favorable to the player because of a much better chance of being
dealt a blackjack, a standing hand of 19 or 20, or drawing a high card
to a hand totaling 10 or 11 with a doubled bet. Also with a shoe rich
in high cards, the dealer has a much better chance of breaking on
a stiff hand (12-16).

My objective was to cut this favorable clump into play. Suppose the favorable one-deck clump was one deck from the top of
the newly shuffled 6-deck stack. When the dealer handed me the
cut card, I would cut one deck from the top and bet big into my
favorable one-deck clump. Mathematically I might have as much
as a 5 to 10% advantage when playing into these favorable
clumps.

By the way, this example also works the other way. Suppose that
the dealer picks up two half-decks to shuffle both containing a
surplus of low cards. This is unfavorable to the player because the
dealer, drawing last, will break much less often than normal. So an
unfavorable one-deck clump is cut out of play. For the example
above, if this one-deck clump is one deck from the top of the newly
shuffled 6-deck stack, the cut is *behind* the one-deck clump. In this
way the unwanted one-deck clump is cut out of play.

Two problems immediately presented themselves in my initial casino testing.

The first involved controlling the cut card. If some other player cuts the newly shuffled stack, he may inadvertently cut your favorable clump out of play or your unfavorable clump into play. So control of the cut card was essential to make the strategy work. This was accomplished in one of two ways: (1) asking for the cut card from whoever the dealer had given it to; or (2) loading up the table with one or more known players or with a team and then signaling to them where the stack was to be cut.

Early in my shuffle-tracking play, I was forced to play off the cut card because I was playing by myself and could not always control the cut card. But this also worked out surprisingly well because if the clump(s) was in the wrong place, this in itself was good information and I could bet the shoe accordingly. For example, if my favorable clump was out of play, I would flat bet (make the same-size bet on each and every hand) the shoe, marking the decks and tracking the shuffle in preparation for the next shoe.

The second problem concerned the shuffle. Not all dealers picked one-half-deck clumps as they shuffled. Some picked quarter-decks. Some picked three-quarters of a deck. To make my tracking accurate, I had to mark the count of the cards dealt in clumps corresponding to their picks.

I perfected my shuffle-tracking method over the next few weeks and practiced marking and tracking for about four hours a day. I practiced for different types of shuffles and different-sized picks. I exchanged ideas with another shuffle-tracking team that Dick was part of. They taught me some simplified methods for marking the count such as using different-colored chips for signifying clumps of high and low cards.

I then recruited a number of my experienced graduates to play with me so I could signal the cuts to them and command total control of the blackjack game. I also played at the same table as Dick's team whenever the opportunity presented itself. These games proved invaluable to me because of "dual tracking." I was tracking, and Eddie, on Dick's team, was using the colored-chip method for tracking. Our cutting agreed most of the time, as did our bet sizes.

This "confirmation" boosted both our confidence levels in our respective methods.

Playing with my recruited graduates and as an ad hoc member of Dick's team, I enjoyed consistent and heavy wins throughout 1981 and into 1982.

There were many successful tracking teams operational in 1981 and 1982: my own, the Czechoslovakian team, Dick's team and a large team operating out of Brigantine, NJ, who apparently learned how to track from the Czech team. Most of the shuffle-tracking data in existence today originated in one form or another with one of these four teams.

The Atlantic City and Las Vegas casinos caught on to the technique in 1983 and changed their shuffles to make it much more difficult to track the clumps.

SHUFFLE-TRACKING IN TODAY'S GAME

Is shuffle-tracking a viable strategy today? Yes, under the proper conditions. You must learn to recognize the characteristics of a "trackable" shuffle, which are described later in this chapter. As mentioned, many Atlantic City and Nevada casinos changed their shuffles to counteract this very effective strategy.

But today things are changing back.

In the fall of 1989 there were three Atlantic City casinos offering trackable shuffles and at least six in Las Vegas. The reader is advised to look for these trackable shuffles and to check out any casino run by inexperienced operators that offer favorable shuffles. There are more and more cases where you can find these, especially on the Indian reservations.

In the world of blackjack, playing conditions run in cycles. The casinos have a tradeoff decision to make in deciding which type of shuffle to employ. They counteracted shuffle-tracking with complicated and time-consuming shuffles that were impossible to track. But they eventually discovered that these shuffles were costing them money in terms of down time—time when the dealer was shuffling and the players were sitting at the table, not losing their money. So do casinos opt to simplify the shuffle, play more hands, maximize profits and take their chances with the shuffle-trackers? Or do they continue to employ the complicated and time-consuming shuffles? If you were a casino manager, what would you do? Very few players have even heard of shuffle-tracking; fewer still know how to track shuffles. Of those who know how to track, a small percentage know enough to do it effectively as a viable moneymaking strategy. Casino managers have finally come to this conclusion and that is why shuffle-tracking is once again a viable strategy.

Is this strategy one that you should learn? To help you decide, let's review the "how-to" description from prior paragraphs in a little more detail. This description assumes you know something about counting cards. If you don't, come back and read this section after reviewing Chapter 2. There is one more point to make before we start. Shuffle-tracking is a complicated strategy, perhaps the most complicated strategy ever developed for winning at blackjack. I will not be offended if you skip over this section and come back to it when you have a broader understanding and decide to incorporate shuffle-tracking into your repertoire of winning tools.

CHARACTERISTICS OF A TRACKABLE SHUFFLE

First of all, the game must be a shoe game; a single- or double-deck game cannot be tracked.

Then there are two prime characteristics that must be present to qualify a trackable game: the type of shuffle employed and the size of the dealer pick.

The ideal shuffle to track is a single shuffle with one-half-deck pick sizes—the dealer breaks the stack—assume six decks—into 2 three-deck piles and shuffles them one time through, "picking" about a half-deck in each hand as the shuffle process is performed.

An example of a shuffle that is difficult to track is the "double shuffle." If the stack is shuffled through more than one time, the game becomes much more difficult to track. In other words, if the dealer breaks the six decks into two stacks of three decks each, shuffles them together, builds up a new six-deck stack, and then repeats this process all over again, the game is probably not trackable and you should not waste your time in trying to.

Pick size refers to the number of cards the dealer "picks" in each hand during the shuffle process. The ideal pick size is one-half deck. But you can track quarter-deck picks up to one-deck picks.

A SHUFFLE-TRACKING PRIMER

Picture yourself sitting at the table, counting down the 6-deck shoe. You have already noticed that the dealer picks up about three-quarters of a deck in each hand when shuffling. (See Learning Drill 10 in Chapter 14 for techniques for estimating deck size.) Starting with the top of the shoe, you are marking the count each ¾s (3Q) deck as the cards are dealt and the hands are played. Suppose the count of the first 3Q is −6. You place a chip on the table in front of you to the 6 o'clock position. You offset it to the left of a base chip to indicate a minus. Suppose the count of the next 3Q is +4. You place a chip in the 4 o'clock position on top of the prior chip and move it slightly to the right of center to indicate a plus.

You continue this counting and marking procedure through the 6-deck shoe until you have a stack of six chips when the cut card is dealt, signaling the dealer that it is time to shuffle. Knowing the count at this spot in the deck, you add two more chips to mark the count of the undealt cards. (Note: Each of the six chips corresponds to one $\frac{3}{4}$ deck clump and add up to $4\frac{1}{2}$ decks. For simplicity we have assumed the dealer deals $4\frac{1}{2}$ decks before shuffling. The last two chips mark the undealt cards in the shoe.)

For example, if your end-of-shoe count is +6, you have 6 extra high-cards in this last clump. But you must mark this count as −6, because this end-of-shoe clump is effectively dealt as the cards are taken out of the shoe and placed in the stack ready to be shuffled. If you don't understand why this end-of-shoe count of +6 is reversed to −6, imagine dealing out this last clump. If you deal it out, with the six extra high cards counting as −1, your count is −6. To simplify the process, remember to mark this last, undealt clump with two chips for the two 3Q-deck clumps; assume each clump is −3.

Charts 1, 2 and 3 illustrate this procedure of marking the count, profiling the discard tray and mimicking the dealer's shuffle process with the chips that represent a clump of cards the size of the dealer's pick during the shuffle process.

There is a simpler version than marking the count with clock positions. Use different-colored chips to mark a "high-card clump" or a "low-card clump." This method was originated by Dick's team, with Eddie providing much of the creative input.

Now what do you do? The stack of chips in front of you is a profile of the cards as they sit in the discard tray prior to the shuffle. You move your chips in the same pattern as the dealer moves the cards. If he breaks the six-deck stack in two piles, you break your stack of chips into two corresponding piles. As he picks up each 3Q deck to shuffle, you pick up two chips, one from each stack, combine them and place them into the new stack in front of you in the same pattern the dealer places the two 3Q deck clumps in front of him as a new $1\frac{1}{2}$-deck clump.

When the dealer finishes shuffling, your chip stack mirrors the new six-deck stack. If the cut is two decks from the end, so is yours; move the bottom two chips to the top of your stack.

CHART 1: TOP VIEW OF CHIP STACK USED TO MARK COUNT OF CARD CLUMPS DURING THE SHUFFLE PROCESS

Top Chip

-3   (3 o'clock position)

-2   (2 o'clock position)

+12 (Use different-colored chip to indicate 12 and 0)

-10 (10 o'clock position)

+1   (1 o'clock position)

-7   (Chip will be positioned to the left to indicate minus
      — see sideview)

+3   (3 o'clock position)

+6   (6 o'clock position)

Bottom Chip

CHART 2: SIDE VIEW OF CHIP STACK

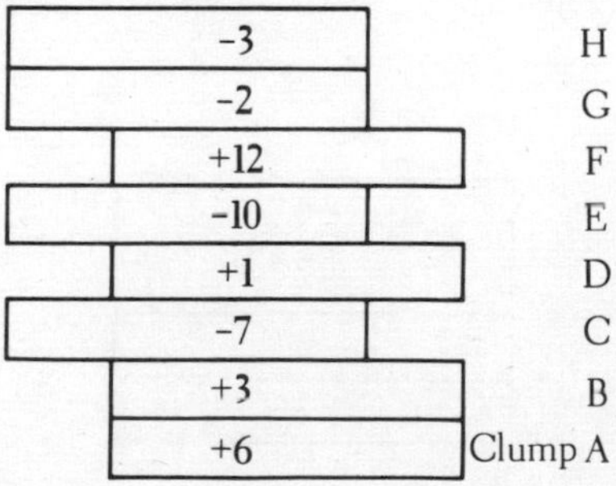

-3	H
-2	G
+12	F
-10	E
+1	D
-7	C
+3	B
+6	Clump A

Note letters designating clumps
Each clump is ¾ (3Q) of 6 – deck stack

CHART 3: USING THE CHIP STACK TO MIMICK THE DEALER SHUFFLE PROCESS

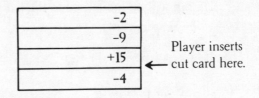

Dealer's first move

The married clumps after the shuffle
Each shuffled deck is ¾ + ¾ = 1½ decks

Player inserts
← cut card here.

The stack after the cut card as it sits in the shoe ready for the next deal. Fifteen unfavorable low cards are cut out of play. Note that the first 4½ decks contain 15 extra high cards (−).

Now what does all this mean? It means that you know, within a half-deck to a deck, where the favorable clumps are and where the unfavorable clumps are in the next shoe. This is very, very powerful information and can provide you with a tremendous advantage over the dealer.

Suppose for example that you have cut a deck and a half to the bottom of the stack that you estimate contains 15 extra low cards and aces as shown in Chart 3. This is equivalent to a count of +15 for the other 4½ decks and can be translated, using simple mathematics, to a player advantage of 5% for this shoe. Your betting strategy, then, is to bet big into these favorable clumps.

The reason you have the edge over the dealer is that high cards, 10s and aces are more valuable to the player than to the dealer. The player can double down (double his bet but draw one and only one more card) on a 9, 10 or 11; the high card helps to win the doubled bet; the dealer, of course, cannot double down. High cards are more favorable on the player blackjack because of the $1\frac{1}{2}$-to-1 payoff (for example a $10 bet wins $15); the dealer collects only even money on his blackjack. And, of course, the extra 10s work against the dealer when he must hit a stiff hand with a higher chance of breaking.

If you are interested in learning how to track shuffles, practice at home for at least fifty hours before trying the technique in the casino. Practice the procedure that I have described above. Cut your favorable clump into play or your unfavorable clump out of play. And then remove this clump from the stack and carefully examine it. How does it compare with what you predicted? If you predicted 15 extra high cards, how many actual high cards are there? If the actual amount is within 25 to 33% of the predicted amount, you have taken the first step. But you are not ready for the casino yet! Will the technique I described above work in a casino? Put the book down now and ponder the next step that you must learn before risking your money in the casino. I never said shuffle-tracking would be easy!

The technique described above will work only if the dealer's pick size is ¾s deck. But what if the dealer picks ½ deck or 0.6 deck? Will the technique work then? No. You have to modify your procedure to correspond to the dealer's pick size and adjust your chip manipulation to simulate the dealer's shuffle.

Before I take you inside my shuffle-tracking blackjack team, operating at the time, and show you exactly how it is done, let me make one suggestion about learning shuffle-tracking and then tell you a story that illustrates the tremendous power that it gives you over the casinos offering trackable shuffles.

First the suggestion: Read and study the team information when you are wide awake and mentally alert; skip ahead if you are in a relaxed mood right now and not in the mood for any heavy, intense reading. Come back to this data at another time when you feel ready to tackle it.

Now the story . . .

There is nothing like the feeling that comes from tracking a shuffle and knowing the "profile" of the next shoe—where the favorable and the unfavorable clumps are. One incident in particular stands out in my memory.

It was December 1981, near Christmas, and my son, Jim, was home for the holidays. We met one of my students, E., a restaurant owner from The Bronx who loved to play blackjack. He joined me every Wednesday night in Bally's for a blackjack play. I had taught Jim the signals for raising his bet and for playing his hand and had bankrolled him, telling him that he was playing to my full bankroll and I would give him 10% of the profits.

I had tracked two high-card clumps and they combined beautifully as the dealer shuffled the decks. I got the cut card and cut this super-rich two-deck clump into play. Both E. and I made a 5-unit bet ($250 for me) right off the top because we knew the high cards were right on top just waiting to be dealt. Jim bet $50, apparently missing my signal. All three of us won as the dealer broke. E. and I continued betting upward of $300 for the next several hands, winning most, with Jim finally nudging out a bet of $100.

By this time I was getting upset with Jim, but I couldn't say too much at the table for fear of giving the game away. The next hand E. and I both bet $500 with Jim holding his bet at $100. Jim is dealt a beautiful blackjack with me pulling a stiff hand. Jim explodes with happiness with his $150 win, not even noticing my break and loss of $500 in his overall excitement. I found out what happened after the session. He froze at the thought of betting anything over $100! Jim did not get his 10% of the profits after that session. But the blackjack hand taught him a valuable lesson when he understood that we lost $350 on the hand ($500 minus his $150 win) when we actually should have won $250 (he should have won $750 with a $500 bet; $750 minus my $500 loss should have been a $250 win). He had no problem in pushing out the chips in the next session.

JERRY PATTERSON'S SHUFFLE-TRACKING TEAM

This is information that I have never published before because of its sensitivity, and I think you will find it quite interesting and extremely useful. I will use Charts 4 and 5 to detail the technique.

Chart 4 illustrates a straight shuffle with 6 decks of cards. At the top third of Chart 4, a 4-pick tracking procedure is detailed. On the left, the 6 decks appear as they would in the discard tray prior to the dealer's initiating the shuffle process. The ¾-deck clumps that are tracked, with 39 cards per clump, are illustrated on the 6 decks, which are numbered 1 to 6 from bottom to top. Notice how every 39 cards is marked off. The shaded areas represent the tracked areas and correspond to the chips in the chip stack illustrated in Chart 1. Be sure you understand this relationship. The chips in your chip stack represent values of the count for each clump of cards marked. In Chart 4 we are looking at a 4-pick shuffle process of 39 cards (3Q deck) per pick.

Still on Chart 4, now notice the middle part of the top third of the chart. The dealer has divided the 6-deck stack into two equal piles with 3 decks in each pile. Notice how the tracked shaded 3Q deck clumps "marry" together as the top three decks in the right-hand figure in the top third of the chart. You have information about two $1\frac{1}{2}$-deck clumps—the top two shaded areas marked "1/4" and "2/5." Suppose "2/5" is your favorable clump, containing 15 extra

CHART 4: SHUFFLE-TRACKING PROCEDURE FOR STRAIGHT SHUFFLE

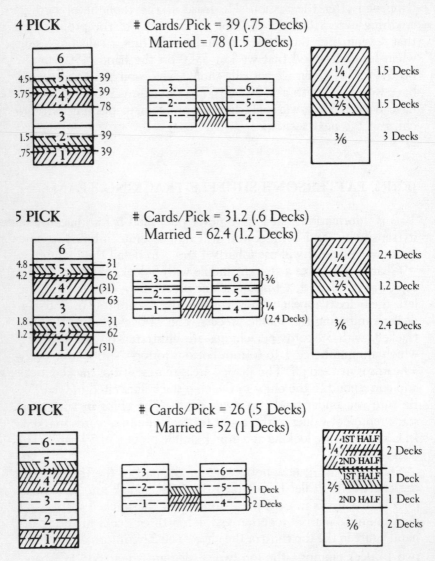

4 PICK   # Cards/Pick = 39 (.75 Decks)
Married = 78 (1.5 Decks)

5 PICK   # Cards/Pick = 31.2 (.6 Decks)
Married = 62.4 (1.2 Decks)

6 PICK   # Cards/Pick = 26 (.5 Decks)
Married = 52 (1 Decks)

Decks 1 & 4 can be tracked as whole decks or as 4 half-decks
(Shaded areas are tracked areas)

CHART 5: SHUFFLE-TRACKING PROCEDURE FOR ZONE SHUFFLE

Dealer's View

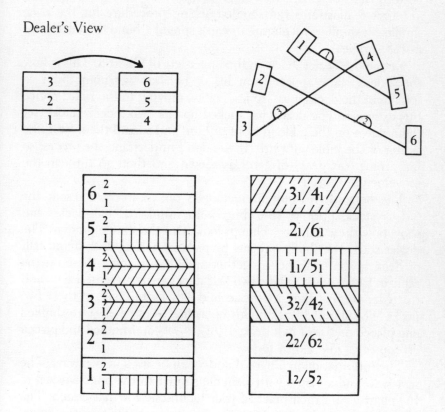

10-value cards and aces. Where do you insert the cut card? Think a minute. The answer is at the bottom of this page.*

Now study the middle third of Chart 4, a 5-pick shuffle process, and the bottom third, a 6-pick shuffle process. In the middle third, do you understand why deck 3 (plus a small part of deck 2), and deck 6 (plus a small part of deck 5) are untracked? Because deck 6, the unseen cards in the discard tray, marries with deck 3. Because of the

---

*The cut card is inserted between "1/4" and "2/5."

unseen cards, this information is not as useful, so there is no need to track deck 3. The same reason holds for the 6-pick process on the bottom third of Chart 4.

Chart 5 illustrates the shuffle-tracking procedure for the zone shuffle—a shuffle with clumps of cards spread around the table prior to the shuffle.

Notice the dealer's view in the upper left of Chart 5. This is how the 2-deck stack appear from his or her vantage point prior to spreading the decks into "zones." Now, moving to the right, notice the six zones. The dealer has picked up the two 3-deck stacks, set them down on the table in front of him, and spread them from the center of the table outward. (If you don't understand the process so far, arrange six decks of cards as shown and then go through the movements yourself.)

The bottom two upright rectangles on Chart 5 represent the 6-deck stack, prior to spreading, with numbered half-decks, and show how these half-deck clumps look after the shuffle process. The dealer starts the shuffle process by picking half of deck 6 and half of deck 1, shuffling them together and then placing them on the table in front of him. These two half-decks are represented as 1_2 and 6_2 to denote that they are the second half, or top half, of these two decks. The shuffled stack builds up as half-decks $2_2/5_2$ are shuffled and placed on top of half-decks $1_2/6_2$, $3_2/4_2$ are shuffled and placed on top of $2_2/5_2$ and so forth.

The information in Charts 4 and 5 can be used in two ways. The first is to find a casino with a shuffle similar to the one analyzed in the charts. And then practice your technique for that casino. The second is to use this data to devise your own shuffle-tracking procedure for the casino of your choice.

Important point: You must document the shuffle of your chosen casino carefully and perform the same detailed analysis shown in Charts 4 and 5. Be sure to notice the pick sizes and the movement of the cards as you document the shuffle. And then do all your analytical work and practice at home. (I am not suggesting you document the shuffle with a note pad in your hand; you must carefully observe the shuffle process, remembering the procedures, and then document it in an unobtrusive place.)

Even though shuffle-tracking is one of the most powerful winning techniques ever devised, it did not represent the pinnacle of the research performed in Pathway 1—the traditional methods. The evolution of blackjack systems and methods continued with the development of an ingenious device—a concealed card-counting computer! The story is told in Chapter 5.

5

Concealed Computers

Imagine yourself sitting at a blackjack table trying to count all the cards as they are dealt. You're in a face-up game and you watch a 6 dealt to the dealer (+1), a pair of face cards dealt to first base (the player on the dealer's immediate left), bringing your running count to −1 (face cards count −1 each), a 10 and a 4 dealt to the next player, leaving the running count at −1 (a 10 at −1 and a 4 at +1 cancel each other out), a 7 and a face card dealt to the next player, yielding a running count of −2 (7s, 8s and 9s are neutral) and on around the table, ending up with a running count of −5.

As the game progresses, you are confronted with a never-ending stream of decisions as each hand is played—converting the running count to a True Count reflecting the players' actual advantage (the True Count is the running count divided by decks remaining to be played—this gives the odds of winning the next hand), betting with the count and playing the hand with the count. All of these arithmetical calculations are done in your head, and it is only natural to get mentally fatigued and make a few mistakes in calculating the count and deciding what to do with it.

Wouldn't it be nice to take a small hand calculator to the table with you to make it easy to keep track of these many calculations? Of course you cannot do this because the pit boss would know that you were counting cards and either bar you from play (Nevada) or ask you to remove the device from the table (Atlantic City).

But imagine yourself wired up with a concealed computer. You are wearing a pair of "magic shoes" that are used to input to the computer the cards dealt. This information is communicated electronically via wires extending up the inside of your pant leg to a miniature computer strapped to the inside of your leg or located in an inside coat pocket. As the computer makes its decisions about bet size and play of the hand, these calculations are communicated to you in a wire running up over your shoulder and down your arm inside your shirtsleeve to a specially constructed watch. But instead of telling time like a normal watch, this watch indicates the decision for betting and playing the hand.

Or you can use an earplug with a voice activator that whispers these decisions in your ear.

Now, to play this game all you've got to do is tap your toes as the cards are dealt. This tells your concealed computer which cards (or card types) have been dealt and, in effect, records the number of cards played throughout the game. Decisions are made automatically and you play effortlessly (although some muscle training is required for the toes).

Sound good? Don't get too excited, because these machines for the most part are no longer available and, more importantly, they are illegal in Nevada. And, if you are caught wearing one in Atlantic City, you are immediately barred from the casino. In Nevada you can go to jail.

To further your understanding of how blackjack systems and methods evolved in the 1980s, I am going to tell you about "Compucount," a concealed computer that I marketed and used.

Let me take you back to May 1983.

I'm sitting at home watching an NBA basketball game with some big money wagered on the outcome. The Lakers and Celtics are battling for the championship. The phone rings and as Nancy goes to answer it I say: "If it's for me, I'm not talking to anybody."

"It's GG", she says. "I don't know any GG", I say, as I watch the Lakers score another basket to hold on to a small lead (my wager is on the Lakers).

"He's got a concealed computer he wants you to market," says Nancy.

Well, that got my attention and I took the call. Thus began a long, friendly and profitable relationship with this most interesting man.

GG had developed a concealed card-counting computer that was less expensive and easier to use than those currently available. Other concealed computers cost as much as $10,000; they were much more expensive to develop and manufacture because they remembered every card. For example, if you were playing in a single-deck game and holding a 16 against a dealer up-card of 6, you would naturally stand and let the dealer hit and, hopefully, break. But suppose there are only five cards left to play; four of them are 5s and the other is a 4. The computer knows this and tells you to hit, knowing you will not break. An optimum decision, giving the player the best odds of winning, was made on each and every hand, depending on the remaining cards to be played. You were playing with a 4 to 5% edge over the house!

GG's concealed computer, which we named Compucount, did not do this, but it cost only $800 instead of $10,000. Furthermore, the voice activator mentioned above cost only an additional $500.

Compucount, using the High-Low Count (2-6 = +1; 7-9 = 0; 10s, face cards and aces = −1), gave you a perfect digital true-count readout on the face of your watch, or a voice readout in your ear device. The True Count could easily be converted to a bet size by betting the True-Count number in units (a betting unit depends on the size of your bankroll; for example, if it's $1000, your betting unit could be defined as $2, $5 or $10 depending on the degree of risk you decide to take) up to a maximum bet, which also depends on the size of your bankroll. For example, if your true-count reading is 5 and your betting unit is $10, you would bet 5 of these ten-dollar units for a bet of $50 on the next hand.

GG and I eventually got together on a deal which called for me to write and publish the Users Manual and develop and implement a marketing strategy. GG in turn would manufacture the devices, work with me in marketing presentations and assist in training the users.

Over the next year we sold over three hundred Compucounts to my clients and by advertising free seminars in *The Los Angeles Times* to the general public and exhibiting Compucount to blackjack players attending these free seminars.

Buyers received training with their purchase for operation and usage. The training sessions became quite humorous. Imagine fifty people, mostly men, in a hotel meeting room, removing their shoes and socks and attaching the toe switches to the balls of their feet. The toe switches had to be positioned to make it as easy as possible to tap the right foot for a high card being played, the left foot for a low card, and both feet together for a neutral card. Some of the initial batch of toe switches didn't work, and a few of our users were running up to the front of the room, sockless, with their pant legs rolled up, exchanging their toe switches.

Then imagine these fifty people running the wires up the inside of their pant legs (the women too) and cutting a hole in the pant pocket, running the wire through that up into the inside pocket of their sport coats, where most wore the microcomputer.

These were hilarious scenes and I'll never forget them.

But these little devices were very reliable and our users got their money's worth because GG guaranteed every machine for defects and replaced toe switches with ones that worked better as the technology advanced. Our users loved the machines, and many went on to win big money by using them in both the Nevada and Atlantic City blackjack games.

It is interesting to note that the casinos didn't discover the existence of these concealed computers until quite some time after they came into use. Kenny Uston, a great blackjack innovator, was the pioneer in their development and successful use. Many interesting stories are included in his book *Million Dollar Blackjack* (reviewed in Part II).

6

Hole-Card Play

Our discussion of the evolution of blackjack systems and methods in the 1980s would be remiss without a discussion of hole-card play. Techniques for reading the dealer's hole card (the down or unseen card) evolved throughout the 1980s, giving the skilled player a huge advantage over those dealers he or she could "read." The more common of these techniques are reviewed in this chapter.

THE "FLASHER"

Picture yourself sitting at the blackjack table. You hold a 16 and the dealer's up-card is a 10. "I wonder what she has in the hole," you think to yourself. "If I knew she had a low card, I would stand on this 16, let her draw and hopefully break."

This is the kind of thinking that led to the research on hole-card play. There are both legal and illegal methods for determining the dealer's hole card. I will discuss the legal methods and mention the illegal ones by indicating their published sources for the interested reader.

The first method is the easiest. Let me take you back to 1984 to describe it.

I'm at a blackjack table in Harold's Club in Reno, seated at the first-base position. I'm playing my hands and winning a little money when I notice how the dealer—her name is Annabelle—is looking at her hole card. Her right hand picks the up card high off the table so that the top of the hole card is visible. She cradles the hole card for a moment while she checks its value, and I can see the card every time!

Now remember this. A dealer peeks under a 10-value card or an ace only to check whether or not he or she has a blackjack.

When Annabelle peeks under a 10 or face card, I know when she has a stiff (a hand totaling 12-16, which could break with the addition of one more card). I can stand on all my stiff hands with a much greater percentage of winning the hands.

I don't hit my 17s, 18s and 19s if the dealer's up-card is a 10-value card and I see a 10 in the hole. Even though the dealer has a 20 and has me beat, if I hit one of these standing hands, it would call undue attention to my play from the pit persons and could tip them off as to what is happening in this very favorable situation. But, if Annabelle "flashes" a low card in the hole, I can now double down on a hand totaling 10 against a dealer up-card of 10 or ace because, although not correct basic-strategy plays, many less-experienced players make these plays, so there is no undue attention called to them.

I get to know Annabelle very well. When she is dealing, I am at first base (the seat to the dealer's immediate left; the first player to receive cards.) And I am playing with very high advantage, perhaps 5% or more. My winnings continue to pile up.

There is only one problem. I am at Reno on a skiing holiday and the fun comes to an end when I have to return to New Jersey. I didn't ski much that year. But all my blackjack trips to Nevada for the next year or two targeted Reno first. Most of my time was spent there before going on to Las Vegas and Laughlin.

I'll never forget, about three years later, I walked into Harold's Club and could not find Annabelle. I checked the bank of pictures on the second floor which exhibit all the employees who have worked in the club five years or longer. Annabelle's picture was no longer there! Checking with a pit boss, I found that she had retired. Annabelle, I still miss you.

I have found "flashers" since, but never one that flashes a perfect picture of the hole card 100% of the time.

Now to answer the important question: Can you still find flashers in today's game? Not very often. Why? Because many of the clubs have changed their rules, forbidding the dealer to peek under the hole card until after all the players' hands have been played. And why is this? Because the casinos have caught on that smart blackjack players have learned how to read hole cards. And how did they catch on? Because of books like *Read the Dealer* by Steve Forte. But more about this later.

THE "CHINESE BLACKJACK"

The second legal method for reading hole cards is called "dealer tells."

You can study some dealers' body mannerisms, called dealer tells, and determine the value of their hole cards. If you are tipping the dealer (see page 127), some will stand back a little, with the cards close to the chest if they are stiff. They subconsciously don't want you to hit. These same dealers will come closer and hold the cards nearer your hand if they are pat (a hand totaling 17-20). Subconsciously, they want you to hit.

Smart blackjack players can learn to spot dealer tells.

The easiest dealer tell to spot is the "double peek." The dealer, in checking under a 10 up-card, peeks once, and then, unsure, peeks a second time. He then proceeds with play because there is no blackjack. Why does he peek twice? Because there is a 4 in the hole. A 4 looks like an ace. The dealer thinks it may be an ace, so he peeks a second time. Orientals call this hand a "Chinese blackjack" because it is the custom for many Orientals to "squeeze" their cards, opening up their two-card hand just a fraction of an inch at a time until the second card comes into view. It's like they are teasing themselves with the mystery of what that second card is. Try squeezing a 4 behind a face card and you will see what I mean—it begins to look like an ace and a blackjack.

If you see a double peek occur, play the dealer's hand for a stiff and stand on your stiff hand. Double if you hold a soft hand, a 9, 10 or 11.

Can you learn to read dealer tells? Maybe. And maybe by the time you read this book, most, if not all of the casinos will have abandoned the practice of allowing their dealers to peek under their hole cards before the players' hands are played.

If you find dealers that still peek, by all means pick up a copy of *Read the Dealer.* (Check my evaluation in Part II of this book, including locations where the book is sold; it is not sold in your neighborhood bookstore.)

"BOATS AND BRIDGES"

The third legal method for reading the dealer hole card is called "reading the warps." This method was first documented in Stanford Wong's *Winning Without Counting.*

The theory is that 10s, face cards and aces tend to bend in the middle when the dealer lifts them up when checking the hole card to determine if the hand is a blackjack. Cards other than 10s and aces tend to bend in the opposite direction because they lie, back to back and facedown against a 10 or ace. These "warps," according to Wong, are readable when they are observed on the dealers' hole cards. Aces and face cards, after warping and when they are dealt as a hole card, look like this: ⌒ . And other cards tend to look like this: ⌣ . (Note: I have exaggerated the warps to make a point. They are not really this pronounced in a real casino blackjack game.)

A friend of mine called the high-card warp a "bridge" and the other card warp a "boat" for obvious reasons.

I recommend you do not try this method; it docs not work in the hand-held games because the cards are changed quite frequently and, in the shoe game, it is difficult if not impossible to get an accurate read. My opinion of his book is neatly summarized by quoting Wong's own words from *Winning Without Counting:* "At most blackjack tables, all the cards have the same warp and thus trying to play the warps is a waste of effort or worse."

The casinos quickly caught on to the method and counteracted it by changing cards in the single-deck games about every hour.

ILLEGAL METHODS FOR READING THE DEALER'S HOLE CARD

"Front loading" may not be illegal but it is borderline cheating and I don't recommend it. To employ this technique, you have to hunch way down in your chair so your eyeballs are almost at table level. Then, when the dealer slides the hole card under the up card, you can sometimes spot its value.

"Spooking" is definitely illegal and is not recommended. It is employed by stationing a confederate, a spook, behind the blackjack table, across the pit. The spook stands in a position that enables him or her to observe the dealer's hole card and then signals its value to his or her partner at the table. This method is further discussed in Kenny Uston's *Million Dollar Blackjack*, which is reviewed later.

The most blatant form of cheating is to form an alliance with the dealer, who will signal you the value of his or her hole card in return for a share of your profits. I strongly advise gamblers to avoid any collusion with any dealer. I advise you the same. You can go to jail if you are caught!

A bizarre method for reading the dealer's hole card occurred several years ago. It involved attaching a microminiature camera to a player's belt buckle and snapping a picture of the hole card as it was dealt. The picture was relayed electronically to a van sitting on the street, outside the casino, which contained state-of-the-art equipment for instantly developing the picture. The value of the picture was then transmitted back to the player at the table. The players involved were caught and tossed in jail. The court ruled that this approach was cheating.

In closing this chapter, let me ask you one favor. If you find a flasher like Annabelle, please call me immediately.

7

All About Biases

So far, in my discussion of the evolution of blackjack systems and methods in the 1980s, I have concentrated on what I defined as Research Pathway 1, or those winning methods based on card counting and other traditional techniques. But there is also Research Pathway 2—a major diversion from Pathway 1 and representing the premise on which this book is based. You were introduced to Pathway 2 in Chapter 2, in which the problems inherent in traditional card-counting methods were identified and the concept of biases caused by the non-random shuffle was introduced. In this chapter, more detail is presented about the Pathway 2 projects, including tips and tactics for short-term players—tips and tactics that you can use on your next trip to the casinos.

LIKE-CARD CLUMPING

Like-card clumping is generally the result of insufficient shuffling or methods intended to minimize the randomness of a shoe or deck.

Such distribution—or lack of distribution—creates an unfavorable game for the skilled player. Sometimes the distribution creates clumps in near-sequential order, and this is why I do not recommend play for at least two hours after new cards are introduced in multiple-deck games.

An exaggerated example of clumping in sequential order would look like this:

* * *

AAA 222 333 444 555 666 777 888 999 XXX JJJ QQQ KKK

Another exaggerated example that illustrates the devastating consequences such clumping creates in multiple-deck games would be a shoe in which all the 10s and face cards—128 in all—were placed at the top, followed by 32 nines, 32 eights, 32 sevens, 32 sixes, 32 fives, 32 fours, 32 threes, 32 deuces and 32 aces.

Obviously, if you were to play this game, the area of the shoe loaded with 10s and face cards would be a virtual standoff between you and the dealer. The rest of the game, however, would be devastating; you would lose the majority of your double-down and pair-split hands and, statistically, the dealer would break less than 28% of the time, which is the average percentage.

EXPERIMENT TO ILLUSTRATE EFFECT OF LIKE-CARD CLUMPING

Take two decks of fresh cards from their boxes and, taking one deck in each hand, execute three shuffles (try to shuffle so as few cards as possible interleave during the shuffle process). Deal the cards to two imaginary players and an imaginary dealer. Play through the two-deck game and observe the effect of like-card clumping. Go through the two decks at the completion of the rounds and inspect the cards as they are spread out in front of you, face-up on the table. Again, take note of the like-card clumping.

You will see clumps or groups of cards that may be somewhat similar to the following example:

K, K, 9, 10, A, 9, Q, 9, J, J, J, 9
8, 6, A, 8, 7, 7, 3, 8, 8, 7, Q, 8.
A, 2, 6, 5, 5, 5, 4, 4, K, 3, 4, 6, 6

Let's take a hypothetical situation in which there are two players against a dealer involved in a game with excessive like-card clumping:

Player 1 is dealt 5-4.

Player 2 is dealt 7-3.

The dealer's up-card is 6.

Player 1 double downs and draws a 6.

Player 2 double downs and draws a 4.

The dealer turns over his bottom card and shows a 5 and then draws a 6 and a 4 for 21 to wipe out the two players.

Let's look at the cards just played:

5, 4, 7, 3, 6, 6, 4, 5, 6, 4

Ten cards were played.

What's the most striking point about the sequence?

There wasn't a single 10 or face card!

If 10s and face cards are equally distributed, one out of 3.25 cards should be a 10 or a face card. This is one of the ways to detect like-card clumping. An abnormal clump of low cards or neutral cards probably means there is an abnormal clump of high cards elsewhere.

When the clump of high cards is too rich, it is not beneficial to the player for the duration of the shoe—only for the hands played in the high-card clump.

HOW TO USE LIKE-CARD CLUMPING FOR TABLE DEPARTURE

Since like-card clumping produces games with extreme plus counts (excessive low cards being dealt) or extreme minus counts (excessive high cards being dealt), this may be your signal to leave the game!

Depart when the count is an extreme minus, dealer-breaking activity subsides, and the game becomes dealer biased. Keep in mind that because of the nature of the shuffle in many shoe games, the distribution will not improve because of the shuffle. What you have done is to detect the beginning of deterioration.

If you are winning and the count is high, play through the high-card clump; however, keep in mind that you are possibly playing in the last shoe of the game—departure is probably near.

While you are in a winning game where high or low card extremes are not evident, be sensitive to small-card clumping that you haven't observed before. Stay in the game, of course, while you are winning; but the observation of unusual clumping is the beginning of a reason to leave. Remember, the shuffle is not likely to improve or dissolve the clumping you have detected.

By being sensitive to like-card clumping, observant players can avoid losing situations. **A winning player understands that he must not only maximize his profits on winning tables but also minimize his loss on losing tables.** Oftentimes, a winning session is saved by avoiding too many losing tables and keeping the profits won from winning tables.

In this section I have discussed how to detect and avoid like-card clumping. Another way to accomplish this is to avoid those casinos where it is most prevalent. The choice of a casino for your blackjack play is a decision that should not be left to chance. Now let me show you. . . .

HOW TO CHOOSE A CASINO WITH A BETTER CHANCE OF WINNING

In a three-year study of the shuffles in the Atlantic City and Nevada casinos, it has been proven conclusively that certain types of shuffles tend to produce, more than others, a higher frequency of dealer-biased tables. A dealer-biased table is one in which the dealer wins more hands than is statistically normal. Conversely, the study proved that other types of shuffles tend to produce, on a comparative basis, more tables that favor the player.

The first tip in choosing a casino is knowing the times to avoid certain casinos. You can dramatically reduce your chances of losing by avoiding play for at least two hours after new cards have been introduced into the shoe game. It is very difficult, if not impossible, to randomly shuffle 8, 6, or even 4 decks of cards. Cards tend to clump in certain patterns that make it extremely difficult to win during this two-hour period. In the Atlantic City casinos, new decks are introduced at 10 A.M., and, in some cases, at the beginning of the swing shift (about 7 to 7:30 on weeknights and 8 to 8:30 on weekends). In the Nevada casinos, new cards are usually introduced into shoe games at the beginning of each shift.

Now let's get into more detail about the choice of casino.

There is a very simple set of tests, easily done by the average gambler, that will indicate whether or not the shuffle will produce more tables that tend to favor the player. Copy down the set of questions below and take them with you when you play blackjack. Mentally ask yourself the questions before you play blackjack. If you get a "yes" to all the questions, do not play blackjack in this casino. Find a better one, because your chances of winning are drastically reduced here.

Here are the questions to answer when evaluating a casino's shuffle:

1. Do the dealers "strip" the cards? (Stripping occurs when the dealer holds about a deck at a time in the left hand and uses the right hand to pick or strip off the cards, a few at a time from the top, middle or bottom, and places them on a new pile.)

2. When the dealer is shuffling, does he pick up *less than 1/2 deck* in each hand to shuffle together? (This action is called "the pick".)

3. Does the dealer alter the shuffle (start stripping, change the size of the picks, increase the frequency of shuffling each stack) after a good shoe in which the players won money?

4. For the wash (the mixing and first shuffle of new decks of cards), does the dealer wash fewer than 4 decks at a time and use the "squeezing" motion mentioned in the Chinese Blackjack experiment to bring about like-card clumping?

5. Does the dealer break the 4-, 6- or 8-deck stack into more than six smaller stacks prior to starting the shuffle procedure?

If your answer to any of these questions is "yes," you should consider very seriously avoiding play in this casino. You will not be getting the best possible game. You can find plenty of casinos in both Nevada and Atlantic City whose shuffles will give you a "no" to all of the above questions. When you are playing in these casinos, you are not, of course, guaranteed a win, but you will get a much better run for your money.

Please be aware that we are not in any way implying that the casinos are doing anything irregular or illegal. The casinos are allowed to shuffle the cards in any way they wish. What these five questions show is "game control," or procedures the casino uses to attempt to disrupt a game in which an excessive amount of money is being won by the players.

It is important to note that not all casinos use game-control techniques. Many players have learned to recognize them and will not play in casinos where they are employed. As a general rule, only some "sawdust joints" (small casinos in Nevada) or larger casinos overly concerned with their bottom line resort to game-control procedures. The existence of these procedures was an important finding of the Pathway 2 research project. Other results are discussed in the next section.

RESULTS OF RESEARCH PROJECT

The major research project in Pathway 2 proved conclusively what we had suspected: that many dealer-biased games occur in high-count situations. This happens because of card clumps produced by certain non-random shuffles. For example, low-card clumps can produce extreme high-count situations. The counter increases his bet in expectation that the missing high cards may appear: a 20 or blackjack or a face card to his doubled 11. But because of extreme clumping, these high cards may not appear in this shoe. Or the high cards may be clumped, many showing up on the same round with most players being dealt 20s and the dealer pulling a 20 also. These high cards are now out of play and not randomly available to the player when one is needed.

We proved that like-card clumping can be devastating to a player. A major reason is that the dealer hits his hand last. The player will stand on a stiff hand, expecting the dealer to break. Playing into a low-card clump, the dealer makes hand after hand, breaking much less often than is mathematically expected.

But we also proved that clumping can be favorable to the player. Many dealer-breaking tables occur on neutral to negative counts. The clump may contain a surplus of rich cards that contribute to the dealer-breaking activity.

The key to winning is learning how to find the favorable player-biased or dealer-breaking games and learning how to avoid the dealer-biased or player-breaking games. The TARGET 21 Method was developed to do just that.

You don't have to analyze or track shuffles to employ the TARGET 21 Method. The method itself will show you how to determine if the game is player-biased and whether or not you should get into the game (or leave the game if the table is deteriorating and the card bias is changing). The method is summarized in the next section.

THE TARGET 21 METHOD

TARGET 21 (*Ta*ble, *R*esearch, *G*rading and *E*valuation *T*echnique) is a proprietary blackjack-table selection method. It is the most significant blackjack tool resulting from Pathway 2 research projects.

TARGET 21 identifies blackjack tables where the players have the advantage over the house. It works because of the non-random shuffle. TARGET 21 players learn to detect the highly favorable player-biased and dealer-breaking tables.

Blackjack research programs have used computers to study the game ever since card counting was invented in 1962. Tens of millions of hands have been played under ideal conditions with a perfect random shuffle. Unfortunately, as mentioned many times in this book, *a random shuffle does not exist in the real world of casino play.* A random shuffle would be difficult for the casinos to implement since even a single deck of cards must be shuffled seven or more times to assure random distribution of the cards.

Research on the effects of the non-random shuffle began in 1982. Much of this research took place inside the casino. By observing and recording thousands of hands, and by simulating thousands more, the project team, with the help of hundreds of my blackjack students, discovered the characteristics of winning and losing tables. This is what we called TARGET 21. It comprises 18 factors that the player uses to evaluate a table. These factors indicate whether or not the table is player-biased or dealer-biased. A player-biased table is one in which, because of favorable clumping, the players will win 50% or more of the hands. A dealer-biased table is one in which, because of unfavorable clumping, the dealer will win 50% or more of the hands.

One of the TARGET 21 factors is the chip tray. To understand how to use this factor, let's assume you to walk into a casino and see four tables in front of you. At three of the tables the dealer's chip tray is full. At the fourth table there are two empty columns with no chips. Which table would you play? Certainly you would select the table with the missing chips, because the players could have won them. But that is not enough by itself, because that winning activity may have happened hours ago and the dealer may be ahead now. It could also mean that players have come to this table, bought chips, played for a while and then left the table, neither winning much nor losing much. But what if the missing chips were won recently by the players? If this is the case, we may have a player-biased game. Of course, this one clue alone is not enough to give you conclusive evidence that this is a player-biased table. The TARGET 21 player uses this factor, in conjunction with 5 or more of the other 18 factors, to decide whether or not this table is an investment opportunity.

(Note: Since TARGET 21 is a proprietary method, I cannot disclose all 18 factors in this book. But I will be happy to send you a 12-page newsletter describing the method in more detail. Use the information request card at the end of this book to contact me. On the other hand, I did decide to publish a proprietary method in this book that exploits short-term opportunities created by the non-random shuffle. In Part III I describe an exclusive method called "TAKEDOWN" for recognizing a TARGET table and for exploiting the short-term opportunities offered by this player-biased or dealer-breaking game. I also included in Part III two other proprietary methods; these help card counters exploit biases caused by the non-random shuffle.)

Here are some other interesting attributes of the TARGET 21 Method:

• Although TARGET 21 can be played without counting cards, it works better if card-counting techniques are employed. But you must use a factor called "table integrity" to decide whether or not to bet up in a high-count situation.

• Card counters enjoy TARGET 21 because it releases them from the constraints of traditional card-counting techniques. No more searching for those elusive games where you play head-to-head against the dealer; no more playing at odd hours when head-to-head games are supposedly available; no more worries about bad cut-card placement; biases detected by TARGET 21 transcend the shuffle, so the effect of cut-card placement is reduced. The TARGET 21 table-entry techniques will get card counters and other blackjack players into many more playable games.

- TARGET 21 is also a short-term moneymaking technique—an important point for the new-era player. It does not work like traditional card-counting techniques, where many hours of play may be required before the mathematics prevail and a player wins money. Through our empirical studies, we have determined that it is possible for TARGET 21 players to win in 70 to 80% of their playing sessions. Table selection is an investment decision. You expect to win at each and every table that you select. When a table does not offer a return on your investment, we teach you to cut short your losses and make a hasty departure: something like a stop-loss technique that is used in stock-market transactions.

- TARGET 21's short-term advantages make it possible to play with a smaller bankroll than is required for traditional card-counting techniques. This is because your chances of winning in any given session are much higher. We have experimented with a $100 casino bankroll and watched it appreciate to $500 on many occasions. The $100 was lost less than one time in five.

- TARGET 21 is a tool that is helpful for high rollers and gamblers even if they do not choose to invest the time to find the player-biased tables. All gamblers need information about when and how much to press their bets no matter at which table they are playing. TARGET 21 gives them this information and provides them with a winning advantage without counting.

There are various styles of play associated with the TARGET 21 Method. Some players scout for biased tables. They use the 18 factors to decide whether or not to sit down and play. Others play at a table with only a few of the factors and, as long as they are not losing, wait for the other factors to develop. Some player-biased tables can be detected one or two shoes before the bias occurs.

Many TARGET 21 players adopt the Partner Play Style. While

one partner plays in a player-biased game, the other scouts for another table in the same casino. If they find a dealer-breaking table, both partners play in the same game.

TARGET 21 works very well in blackjack tournaments. You can't choose your table in a tournament, but you can use the TARGET factors for your betting and playing decisions. One TARGET player won a recent tournament in Las Vegas, claiming more than $56,000 in prize money. Many others have placed quite high.

BLACKJACK QUIZ

If you answer "yes" to any of the questions below, you should consider taking advantage of the moneymaking opportunities of the TARGET 21 Method.

Have you ever sat at a blackjack table where the dealer was breaking a lot and you could do no wrong? You kept beating the dealer hand after hand?

Were you ever $100 or more ahead while playing blackjack but did not leave the table when the cards turned against you? You gave back all your profits and then some?

As a card counter, have you ever lost hand after hand in a very high-count situation with your maximum bet out and seen your trip's profits go down the tubes?

Have you ever won hand after hand with your minimum bet out? How much more would you have made if you could have known the dealer would keep on breaking?

Are you a would-be card counter who practiced at home but could never master counting? Does winning without counting appeal to you?

Have you ever watched a blackjack player making a tremendous amount of money with seemingly little effort? Picture yourself in his or her shoes, taking the money off the table. With TARGET 21, this is possible.

If you are interested in finding out more about TARGET 21, please see Chapter 22 for an outline of my TARGET 21 Instructional Program.

8

Summary and Conclusions for Today's Player

To end my discussion on the evolution of blackjack systems and methods in the 1980s, I will pose and answer a number of questions that you may be asking at this point in the book:

- Can blackjack be beaten in today's environment?
- Which overall strategy should I adopt?
- Should I learn how to win from a book or go to a school?
- Should I learn how to count cards or is there a more effective way to win better suited for today's blackjack environment?

I can answer a few of these questions now and the remainder will be answered as this book unfolds.

Yes, blackjack can still be beaten. But it is not as simple as it was in the '80s when blackjack players could learn a point-count system, a basic playing strategy, and money-management betting tactics. You have to recognize two realities of today's game:

1. For reasons already discussed, the count does not always work. You must learn when to use a count system and when not to. I will teach you how to do this later in this book.

2. Even if the count would always work against today's game, the

pit bosses have become very adept at spotting card counters by their betting patterns. In Atlantic City, where state regulation prohibits the casinos from barring gamblers, pit bosses can either restrict a player's betting spread (the ratio between a big bet when the count is high and a small bet when the count is low) or shuffle up (shuffle and restore the cards to a new deck or new shoe to effectively remove the player's advantage) on a player if his or her betting spread becomes too high. In Nevada a person detected as a card counter or thought to be a card counter may be barred from play.

The decision on what strategy to adopt can be made with information you acquire from this book. I will help you make this decision. If you learn how to count, it should become one of a number of winning tactics you employ.

Some of the strategies discussed in Part I are not suitable for today's environment. Shuffle-tracking can be employed only in those instances where the shuffle can be tracked; many cannot be tracked. Hole-card play is already an endangered species because of the material now available in Steve Forte's *Read the Dealer* (reviewed in Part II). Few dealers peek under their up card, and the number of games where the dealers peek is growing smaller with each passing year. Concealed computers, as noted, are an anachronism and illegal in today's game.

Team play is still a very usable and profitable technique if you have the necessary management and communication skills coupled with trustworthy players.

The first major decision you must make is, should you treat blackjack as a short-run or long-run game?

If you decide to become a traditional player and treat blackjack as a long-run game, you will accept the mathematics of card counting and not be too concerned with short-term table biases caused by the non-random shuffle. I will recommend to you the most effective card-counting system and teach you the correct basic strategy and how to bet with the count; all the information you need is contained in Chapter 14—A Handbook of Card Counting Drills.

But if you decide to treat blackjack as a short-term game, as I do, I will teach you when card counting should be used and when it should not. *Playing on the Run, Count Reversal* and the *High-Low*

Plus strategies discussed in Chapter 15 all resulted from Research Pathway 2 but, even if you are a traditional player, I believe these methods will be of interest to you and aid you in your quest to become a consistent, winning player.

I will teach you a non-counting method for exploiting a favorable bias should such a bias develop at your table. The TAKEDOWN Method discussed in Chapter 13 also resulted from Research Pathway 2.

However, before I get to these methods in Part III, it is important for you to review and understand the information that is available to you right now. You need to know which books, courses, schools and newsletters are worth your time and which are not. I will review and evaluate current blackjack learning information in Part II.

PART TWO

Review and Analysis of Available Information

9

Blackjack Books

CRITERIA FOR EVALUATION

From my teaching experience over the past twelve years, I estimate that over 90% of all blackjack players who seek more information about how to win first acquire a book. Since many players go no further in finding instruction, it is important for this book to point them in the right direction.

The evaluations below are structured for both the traditional player and the new-era player. I defined the traditional player in Chapter 1 as one who accepts the mathematics of the game, who accepts the computer-derived strategies based on a random-number generator, and who plays for the long run. The new-era player was defined as one who recognizes the realities of short-term play and who learns to exploit the short-term opportunities engendered by biases in the non-random shuffle—the "real-world" shuffle executed by dealers at blackjack tables in casinos.

Some of the books that I evaluate are worthwhile for traditional card counters but would be of no value whatsoever to the new-era player. This difference is indicated in the category definitions and in the evaluations of various books.

I have divided my review and evaluation of blackjack books into the following categories:

Category 1: Top rated, must contain a wealth of data, some not found in any other book; contains a practical and usable method and learning aids for that method; belongs in every player's library.

Category 2: Contains some useful and practical information; interesting reading; belongs in all traditional players' libraries; may be of some interest to new-era players.

Category 3: Contains some useful information for traditional players but of little use to new-era players; not mandatory reading; players wanting a complete blackjack library may wish to acquire.

Category 4: Just another blackjack book, no reason for buying it, possesses little or no practical value; may contain obsolete data; probably contains data duplicated in other blackjack books.

Some books reviewed in these four categories are difficult to find in your local bookstore because they were published by a small publisher. This will be indicated. Sources for purchasing these books are identified and listed in a later chapter.

The pocket-sized books that explain how to play blackjack and offer simple strategies are not reviewed.

The definition of these categories and the placement of books within each category is done subjectively and is strictly the author's opinion based on thirty-four years of blackjack play and research.

Not all blackjack books are included in this review—only those germane to accomplishing the goals established for this book. The omission of a book should not be construed by the reader to mean that it has no practical value.

To satisfy the reader's curiosity I will indicate, where known, what each of the book's authors is doing today as this book is written.

Prices shown for each book are subject to change.

And finally, to be fair, I have not reviewed any of my own blackjack books. I leave it to the reader to be the judge.

CATEGORY 1 BOOKS

• Braun, Julian H. **How To Play Winning Blackjack.** Chicago: Data House Publishing Co., 1980, $12.95.*

I met Braun in 1964 at the Fall Joint Computer Conference in Las Vegas. He and I were appearing as speakers at a seminar on

*Now out of print but available from Gambler's Book Club; 630 S. 11th St., Las Vegas.

"Using Computers to Beat Games of Chance and Skill," chaired by Dr. Ed Thorp (inventor of card counting). Braun had performed all the computer work for Thorp's Ten Count System. It was quite interesting that Thorp and Braun, the two big guns of blackjack research, did not take center stage. Harvey Dubner, an unknown engineer, used the conference to announce his High-Low Point-Count System. Since Thorp's Ten Count System was extremely difficult to learn, let alone play in the casino, Dubner was the hit of the seminar and was mobbed by the overflow crowd afterward for copies of his paper.

Braun and Thorp were also excited about the possibilities of High-Low, and Braun went on to do all of the computer work to compute True-Count values for correctly playing the hands by using the count. The mathematically derived basic strategy for playing each blackjack hand against a given dealer up-card is described in Chapter 20. But skilled players know that most hands can be played according to the count. For example, the correct basic-strategy play for a player hand totaling 16 against a 10 up-card is hit. But if you are counting, you have learned to stand on a count of zero or above and hit on any negative count.

Braun has since performed every major computer study involved with computing and refining the basic playing strategy and modifying this strategy with the High-Low Count.

Most of this work was done before he published *How to Play Winning Blackjack*. The book is classic and timeless. It not only defines basic strategy but shows you graphically and in color why each hand is played the way it is. Braun's book is highly recommended to help you learn the basic strategies presented in Chapter 20.

But the book is more than a treatise on basic strategy. Braun recognizes the value of discipline and the advantage to the player of departing a losing table. He also sensed that there were cycles in the game, and is the first author I know of to comment on their occurrence. He offers no method for exploiting them other than the generalities of betting up when you are winning and backing off when you start to lose. How do you know when these winning and losing cycles occur? "Develop that sixth sense," he advised. "Sensitivity is a developed skill." These words, although general in nature, gave me some of my reasons for doing research that ultimately led to the development of the TARGET 21 Method.

Basic strategy is the foundation of your game, and learning it will be made much easier by reading Braun's book, which explains the simple arithmetic behind each play.

Julian Braun works for the IBM Corporation in Chicago.

• Forte, Steve. **Read the Dealer.** Berkeley, CA: RGE, 1986, paper-bound, $40.

This is a book that contains such powerful data and strategies that I wish it had never been published (see why below). It teaches you how to determine the dealer's hole card by reading "tells," or dealer body-language, that subconsciously signals the value of the hole card to the knowledgeable player.

Forte holds nothing back and writes about basic "tells" for hitting and standing, "verbal" tells, "ghost" tells, "break-in" tells, "strong-arm" tells and many others. He also includes a strategy for playing the hands when you have this information.

This book gives you invaluable data for capturing a big advantage over the casino.

My only question is: Why did he publish it, knowing that its very existence would give the casinos the same data and force them to change the procedures that allowed the dealers to peek at their hole cards? Since the book's publication in 1986, over half of the Nevada casinos have already changed their policies. (In Atlantic City, from the beginning, the dealers did not peek at their hole cards.) More and more casinos are changing to the no-peek procedure as time goes on. Wouldn't you if you owned a casino? Why give anybody an advantage over your game?

So why did Steve Forte publish this data and negate one of the most powerful winning tactics yet devised? Sure, he wasn't the first to write about tells; Ian Andersen and Stanford Wong mentioned them briefly in their books. But neither published the very elaborate methods for reading the tells that Forte did.

You should know that this book costs $40 and you must order it from a gambling bookstore. (Note: Gambler's Book Club in Las

Vegas sells it.) It is not available from your local bookstore. The tell-reading methods are also difficult to learn and take many, many hours of practice. These techniques are more suitable for professional players than recreational ones. If you want to give it a try anyway, contact me after completing this book and I'll let you know if any casinos are left where the dealers still peek at their hole cards.

• Uston, Ken. **Million Dollar Blackjack**. Hollywood, CA: SRS Enterprises, 1981, paperbound, $14.95.

If you are a traditional card-counter or plan to become one, this book is for you. A veritable handbook of card-counting techniques together with practice routines, it leads the reader on a step-by-step program for learning the basic strategy for playing the hands, a simple Level I count and, for those up to it, Uston's Level III Advanced Point-Count System.

Uston gives excellent instruction on betting strategies, multiple- and single-deck play and blackjack team methods. His chapters on front loading, "spooking" and cheating are fascinating.

But the best part of the book, in my opinion, is the chapters on his own teams: their formation and their operation including the successes and failures.

It is a best-seller and it is the book read by over 90% of the players who call me for instruction. Even if you never learn how to count cards, it is must reading and belongs in your blackjack library.

An interesting footnote to this evaluation is that Uston may have been the first player to recognize card clumping and its effect on the player's chances of winning. He discusses a game he got into several years ago in which new cards were introduced into play. To quote: "As we began play, I couldn't believe how the cards were coming out. Seven of the first ten cards were 4s. Then, a batch of 3s came out, followed by a group of 6s; then, a clumping of 10s and aces. I kept track of the count, which soared astronomically, as more little cards came out. Staying at $25 minimum bets, I lost hand after hand."

What Uston is discussing here is a game with an insufficient wash and the devastating effects of like-card clumping.

Ken Uston is deceased.

CATEGORY 2 BOOKS

• Canfield, Richard Albert. **Blackjack Your Way to Riches.** Secaucus, NJ: Lyle Stuart, 1977, paperbound, $9.95.

I've met Richard Canfield only once but that was *not* enough. Former pit boss, raconteur, blackjack player, he is truly a character right out of Damon Runyon. His book discusses the usual run-of-the-mill topics of interest to traditional blackjack players: basic strategy, card counting, money management, how not to get barred from casinos—but with one important difference. He is an excellent writer, tells a great story and has a marvelous sense of humor. His is the kind of book you pick up and cannot put down. Canfield organizes his book well and uses sidebars liberally.

There's not much that's new, but if you're a student of the game, this is a book you will want to have.

Richard Canfield is retired.

• Humble, Lance, and Cooper, Carl. **The World's Greatest Blackjack Book.** Garden City, NY: Doubleday & Co., 1980. Revised edition, 1987, paperbound, $9.95.

This is an excellent book for the traditional blackjack player. It covers the game from A to Z, with a thorough description of basic strategy and card counting. It touches on the psychological side of the game and makes the player aware that he must gain control of his emotions if he is to become a consistent winner.

Humble incorporates his own card-counting system, called Hi Opt I, into the book. Previously marketed for $100, the system compares favorably with other card-counting systems, on paper and in computer runs. However, it is extremely difficult to obtain this computer advantage in the casino. This is because Humble values the ace as 0 in his point-count assignments. Therefore, to work to theoretical efficiency, the counter must keep a side count of aces and factor this in to the betting decision. This is just not feasible in the real world of casino play.

The book gives the player good advice on how to stay away from "hot" dealers, although the authors' reasons for this may be faulty.

They write about the possibilities of cheating, but they don't address the more probable reasons for table biases. In my experience there is little cheating in casinos today. Sure, there may be a "mechanic" (a dealer who can manipulate cards to his or her own advantage during the shuffle) or two that ply their trade, but if they exist at all, they are anachronisms. The casinos don't have to cheat to take the typical gambler's money. They have the odds and shuffles working for them. If they do find cheating dealers, they fire them on the spot. Furthermore, most games dealt are shoe games, which makes it much more difficult to cheat. And finally, the turnover among dealers is high. Chances are when you sit down to play, even in a hand-held game, your dealer is working with one or two years' of experience or less—not nearly enough time to learn the tricks of the mechanic.

Nevertheless, there are some very interesting blackjack stories in this book. The most interesting are those about Lawrence Revere and his trips to Toronto (Lance Humble's home city) and joint play, with Lance and his friends, in the private games that Humble introduced him to. These alone are worth the price of the book.

Lance Humble is a professor at a Toronto university.

Ken Cooper is head of his own company in a non-gambling field.

• Roberts, Stanley (with Edward O. Thorp; Lance Humble, Ph.D.; Julian Braun; Jerry Patterson; Arnold Snyder; Ken Uston; D. Howard Mitchell). **The Gambling Times Guide to Blackjack.** Publisher: Gambling Times, Hollywood, CA, 1984. Distributor: Lyle Stuart Inc., Secaucus, NJ, paperbound, $5.95.

To my knowledge his book is the first to contain a workable shuffle-tracking technique, a method for tracking the undealt cards (those remaining in the shoe when the cut card comes out) through the shuffle and into the next shoe.

The book is also the only blackjack book in existence to feature winning ideas from all the great blackjack minds of the 1970s and 80s; it's an eclectic collage of winning tips and ideas.

Uston's contributions on team play and comments on what to do if you are barred from play, and Roberts' contributions on bankroll management, how to become an expert player and tournament play are especially interesting.

Stan Roberts is head of a direct mail and publishing company.

• Uston, Ken. **Ken Uston on Blackjack.** Secaucus, NJ: Lyle Stuart Inc., 1986, hardbound, $16.95.

In the summer of 1985 I was teaching a blackjack class at the Jockey Club in Las Vegas when I saw Kenny Uston for the last time. He had shaved his beard and straightened his hair. He looked just like his pictures when he was vice president of the Pacific Stock Exchange. When I saw him I knew him right away, even though his new appearance was a disguise to fool the casinos.

Kenny had organized and was managing his last team at the time. The adventures of this team were documented in his book, *Ken Uston on Blackjack.* I couldn't wait to get a copy.

It contains fascinating stories, and Uston holds nothing back about his unique Team Play techniques, including a team-play adventure with a concealed computer. The reader will also find interesting Uston's barrings and legal machinations in the Nevada courts to try to regain his right to play blackjack without getting barred.

This is a classic and timeless book that made a major contribution to blackjack literature.

CATEGORY 3 BOOKS

• Andersen, Ian. **Turning the Tables on Las Vegas.** New York: Vanguard, 1976, paperbound, $4.95.

This is the first book to address the problems of getting barred for counting cards. It discusses camouflage techniques for getting friendly with the pit bosses and dealers, and fooling them into thinking that you are just another average losing gambler. Andersen recommends tipping the dealer and playing up to the dealer's ego to receive the most favorable playing conditions, for instance, deeper deck-penetration to maximize the player's advantage as a card counter.

The book sold very well when it was first published in 1976 because the data in it was very usable in the conditions existing at that time. However, it is not all that useful in today's game because most pit bosses have caught on to all of Andersen's tricks. It should be mentioned that this is the first book that discussed the art of tell playing.

If you are a traditional card counter and want to learn how to camouflage your play, you still should get some pretty good ideas from this book. And it does make very interesting reading.

Ian Andersen is a professional investor.

* Chambliss, C. R., and Roginski, T.C. **Playing Blackjack in Atlantic City.** Las Vegas: GBC Press, 1981, paperbound, $9.95.

The two authors did a very thorough mathematical and computer analysis of the Atlantic City Game shortly after the casinos opened there. It will now interest only traditional card counters with a mathematical background who want to know about the game as it existed at that time.

The two authors are mathematicians working for a firm in the Pennsylvania area.

* Einstein, Charles. **Basic Blackjack Betting.** Las Vegas: GBC Press, 1980, paperbound, $2.95.

This is a good book and has some interesting data on "streak theory," namely, the theory of winning multiple hands in succession. The author should be commended for developing the first workable non-count betting system and backing it up with an interesting analysis based on laboratory data.

Unfortunately, the system (bet small until you win; then bet big until you lose, with variations) never really caught on and was never verified to my satisfaction with live data from real world play in the casinos.

* Griffin, Peter A. **The Theory of Blackjack.** Las Vegas: GBC Press, 1979. 4th Revised Edition published in Las Vegas: Huntington Press, 1988, paperbound, $9.95.

This is an excellent book if you understand probability theory, mathematics and statistics. The author's wit and theoretical knowledge of the game are very evident in between the complex statistical formulas. It is unfortunate that he couldn't translate more of his formulas into words that the average player can understand.

• Malmuth, Mason. **Blackjack Essays.** Self-published 1988, paperbound, $19.95.

Just what the title implies. It is of interest mainly to traditional card counters.

Mason Malmuth is a poker player.

• Revere, Lawrence. **Playing Blackjack as a Business.** Secaucus, NJ: Lyle Stuart Inc. Fifth Revised Edition 1980, paperbound, $14.95.

This book was the card counter's Bible for a number of years. Published originally in 1971, it contains beautiful basic-strategy charts in color and descriptions of four of the counting systems Revere developed with the assistance of Julian Braun. I first read this book in 1977 when I was doing the research for the initial, self-published edition of my blackjack book. I remember devouring Revere's book from cover to cover and being extremely impressed with the work he and Braun had done. In fact, *Playing Blackjack as a Business* served as the basis for the Simplified Basic Strategy published in the original editions of my book. Now, of course, *Playing Blackjack* has been rendered obsolete by many succeeding books and is of mainly historical interest.

Lawrence Revere was a colorful character, a demanding instructor, a creative system-developer and a winning player. As a former pit boss and with many casino connections, he was active on both sides of the table. There have probably been more stories told about him than any other blackjack player. You can find very interesting ones in Humble's *The World's Greatest Blackjack Book*, as previously noted.

I never had the opportunity of meeting Lawrence Revere, who passed away in 1977. I wish I had.

• Roberts, Stanley. **Winning Blackjack.** Hollywood, CA: SRS Enterprises, 1981, paperbound, $95.

This book is pricey at $95 a copy. It contains solid instructional data, and the system it recommends works well in the single-deck game. However, with the ace valued as +1 along with all the other cards from 2 through 9 (the 10s and face cards are valued as −1), I would not recommend using this point-count system in a shoe game.

The book has an excellent section with illustrations about cheating, good advice on money management and practical tips from a professional player.

• Snyder, Arnold. **Blackbelt in Blackjack.** Berkeley, CA: RGE, 1983, paperbound, $12.95.

This is Arnold Snyder's version of a basic blackjack book, including tips on how to play, basic strategy, card counting and money management. Snyder has incorporated his own card-counting systems, which are no better and no worse than systems covered in many other books reviewed in this chapter.

His attempt at innovation includes the introduction of a strategy called "depth charging." This strategy is designed for the single-deck game. In a game with three or more rounds dealt before the shuffle, the player skilled enough to execute this strategy has an advantage of 0.79% in Las Vegas and 0.26% in northern Nevada.

This strategy involves flat betting, or using a betting strategy not related to the count and using the True Count to play the hands. The strategy may be suitable for professionals with many hundreds of hours of practice using the True Count to make play variations, but for the occasional player it is just not feasible.

Snyder also introduces a strategy called "opposition betting" that makes at least a couple of pages interesting to new-era players. In this strategy, which involves waiting for the count to turn down before raising the bet, Snyder gets right to the borderline of understanding the effect of card clumping on today's game. In fact, there could not be a better example of the devastating effect of like-card clumping than the letter from one of Snyder's clients which he prints on page 86. This letter is from a counter who kept losing in shoe after shoe because the count kept going up and never coming down, i.e., this counter was playing into a low-card clump with the high cards never coming out to provide the card counter's theoretical advantage.

Snyder's comments to this client as published on page 87 are: "Such a clumping of cards could occur purely through chance or possibly due to a poor shuffle." He then goes on to advise this client that "this is not going to be a beatable game."

Snyder's solution as written in 1983 is to track the undealt cards in the shoe through the next shuffle. It's unfortunate that he didn't recognize the much simpler solution of table departure! If you ever find yourself in a shoe like this, please don't follow Snyder's advice; follow mine and leave the table.

Snyder, a postman during the day and a blackjack researcher and newsletter publisher at night, should spend more time doing his research in the casinos instead of on computers. The aforementioned letter gave him all the reasons he needed to do some research in the real world of casino play. He missed the whole point by recommending shuffle-tracking as a solution. I will have more to say about Snyder, the so-called "gadfly of blackjack," in my chapter on newsletters.

* Snyder, Arnold. **The Blackjack Formula.** Berkeley, CA: RGE. Revised 1982, paperbound, $10.00.

This book contains a formula for computing the player's advantage in a blackjack game depending on the rules of play, the decks in the game and a few statistical factors about the point-count system being employed. Snyder sold the book for $100 a copy when it was first published. Now he sells it for $10. Just one more strong indicator that the game has changed and that cardcounting does not work as well today as it did ten years ago.

* Thorp, Edward O. **Beat the Dealer.** New York: Random House, 1962. Revised version, New York: Vintage Books, 1966, paperbound, $5.95.

This is the book that started it all with the publication of the first card-counting method for beating the game of 21. The original edition was published in 1962, and contained a strategy for counting

10s and "others" (all other cards). This system turned out to be extremely difficult to use in casino play. Card counting for the masses never really caught on until the second edition of Thorp's book was published in 1966. This included Harvey Dubner's High-Low Point Count System, with basic strategy variations calculated by Julian Braun.

There were many other winning tactics published in this remarkable book, including a method for counting aces and 5s. But the most interesting of these tactics is the one which involves "end play." In the old days, the casinos dealt the deck right down to the bottom, dealing out either 51 or all 52 cards. A counter had a tremendous advantage near the end of the deck because he or she knew what was left to play. Thorp uses an interesting example with just seven cards left to play. Suppose they are all 10s and aces. You are in a head-to-head game and now spread to three hands. You are dealt six of these favorable 10-value cards and aces, leaving the last one for the dealer. Your three hands all contain either 20 or blackjack. The dealer must shuffle and draw from the new deck containing extra low-cards. You have a tremendous advantage.

So, if you are curious about why the dealer shuffles about two-thirds of the way into a single-deck game, now you know one of the most important reasons: to prevent end play.

If you buy this book, and I recommend that you do, try to find a copy of the original hardbound edition published in 1962 by Random House. In the 1966 edition the publisher had to cut some of the most interesting parts out of the original edition to make room for the section on the High-Low Point Count. Call one of the gambling bookstores mentioned in Chapter 23.

Ed Thorp is a professional investor and money manager.

- Wong, Stanford. **Professional Blackjack.** Chicago: William B. Morrow & Co., 1981, hardbound, $19.95.

When this book was first published in 1977, it revolutionized the way card counting was employed to gain an advantage at the blackjack table. Prior to this book, the standard way to play was to sit down at a blackjack table, keep a running count of the cards and make small bets when the count was low and the dealer had the advantage and large bets when the count was high and the player had the advantage. Wong changed all that, and in so doing even added a word to the blackjack player's lexicon—"Wonging it." Wong's approach involved keeping a count behind the table without sitting down and therefore without playing any hands disadvantageous to the player. This was called "back counting." The player entered the game only when he had the advantage, leaving once again when the count turned negative and favored the dealer. In this way the player was making flat bets and not following the usual up-and-down betting patterns of the typical counter.

It took the casinos two or three years to catch on to this method and implement countermeasures. In many cases the dealer is instructed to shuffle up or restrict the player's bet size to table minimum until the shuffle. Of course, this countermeasure is taken only if a player is obviously standing behind the table, waiting for a high count to occur.

Wong is to be commended for adding an innovative and winning tool to the blackjack player's arsenal. It's just too bad it's out-of-date.

Stanford Wong publishes a blackjack newsletter (reviewed in Chapter 10) and is a professional blackjack tournament player and a professional videopoker player.

• Wong, Stanford. **Winning Without Counting**. La Jolla, CA: Pi Yee Press, 1978, hardbound, $24.95.

Out of 237 pages in this book, 50 are devoted to playing the warps and 10 are devoted to tells. My review of Wong's data on warps, as published in *Break the Dealer* (coauthored with Eddie Olsen) states: "Wong claimed remarkable success . . . with warped cards. 'I am right about 65% of the time when I think the hole card is 2 through 9,' Wong wrote. He even compiled more than 30 pages of variations based on his guesswork. For players whose calculations didn't correspond with Wong's, he provided an appendix with the appropriate variation numbers. For example, if you were right 49% of the time at calling 10s and aces, you could go ahead and hit a hard 17 against a dealer's 8 up-card. But you had to be able to guess correctly 64 percent of the time before you could hit a hard 17 against a 10 up-card."

The review from *Break the Dealer* goes on: "There's no mathematical basis for reading warped cards. And even Wong conceded that the technique of reading warps in cards is sometimes ineffectual: 'At most blackjack tables, all the cards have the same warp and thus trying to play the warps is a waste of effort or worse.'"

Wong includes 10 pages of detailed information about how to cheat at the blackjack table. The comments from my review: "If such guesswork didn't work out, Wong included other noncounting methods—better known as 'cheating.' One such method was to substitute the cards dealt to you with your own cards. 'Be careful to match color and casino name exactly,' Wong wrote. In other words, don't replace El Cortez cards with Circus Circus cards. He also advised, 'I strongly recommend that you not get caught cheating.' We, on the other hand, strongly recommend that you do not cheat."

This book received good reviews when it was first published in 1978 and sold for $200. It now sells for just $25, which is a better reflection of the value contained therein.

CATEGORY 4 BOOKS

Be careful if you buy any of these books. Many contain obsolete and/or inaccurate data. None are recommended.

- Black, Jack. **The Card-Counting Guide to Winning Blackjack.** Kings Park, NY: Consumer Publications, 1983.
- Cardoza, Avery D. **Winning Casino Blackjack for the Non-Counter.** Santa Cruz, CA: Cardoza School of Blackjack, 1981, paperbound, $4.95.
- Chin, Kenneth S.Y. **Understanding and Winning Casino Blackjack.** New York: Vantage Press, 1980, out of print.
- Dubey, Leon B. Jr. **No Need to Count.** New York: A. S. Barnes & Co., 1980, paperbound, $5.95, out of print.
- Patrick, John. **So You Wanna Be a Gambler.** Metuchen, NJ: John Patrick, 1983, paperbound, $9.95.

- Popik, David O. **Winning Blackjack Without Counting Cards.** Secaucus, NJ: Citadel Press, 1985, paperbound, $7.95.
- Silberstang, Edwin. **Playboy's Guide to Casino Gambling: Blackjack.** New York: Wideview Press, 1980, out of print.
- Tulcea, C. Ionescu. **A Book on Casino Blackjack.** New York: Van Nostrand Reinhold, 1982, paperbound, $8.95.

10

Other Available Information

Other information reviewed falls into four categories:

- Blackjack Newsletters
- Blackjack Study Courses, Schools and Learning Aids
- Consultation/Advice From Blackjack Experts
- The Gambler's Book Club

BLACKJACK NEWSLETTERS

Four blackjack newsletters are reviewed in this section. Each has been around for two years or more and has published an issue within the last ninety days. Each publishes information mainly on blackjack.

- **Blackjack Forum** by Arnold Snyder: four issues at $30 per year. RGE Enterprises, Berkeley, CA.

Snyder states many times in the pages of his newsletter that only a handful of players are capable of beating the game as it is played today. One wonders, then, just what purpose is served by *Blackjack Forum*.

Much of *Blackjack Forum* is dedicated to computer studies of card-counting issues such as: Which point-count system has the greatest betting efficiency? What effect does dealing deeper into the deck or shoe have on the player's overall winning advantage? What is the win rate of a 4-to-1 betting spread (ratio between your high bet and low bet) when you jump from a bet of 1 to 4 as opposed to a 4-to-1 betting spread when you take a middle step, raising your bet from 1 to 2, to get there? In how many hands out of 100 will the player have a 2% advantage in a single-deck game? Double-deck game? Etc.? And so on and so forth.

If you are into frequency distributions and statistical analyses, you will love *Blackjack Forum*.

Now I am not disputing that this data may be of value to a certain breed of blackjack player. But the fact is we are dealing with a game with a mathematical advantage to the player in the 1% range. A mistake or two in the count, or just a simple statistical fluctuation, easily wipes out this 1% edge that the player supposedly enjoys.

This critique of Snyder's *Blackjack Forum* gets right to the root of our discussion of new-era player (short-run) vs. traditional player (long-run).

Let me quote from one of Snyder's recent issues, and you can judge for yourself whether or not this data is of any interest to you: "A simplified 'average' counting system, such as the High-Low employing strategy indices from −1 to +6 only, shows an advantage of +.01%, very close to a perfect break even with the house, using a 1-to-2 spread in the 4-deck strip game with a 75% shuffle-point."

I must admit to being impressed with Snyder's loyal band of readers. One reason this newsletter appeals to traditional card counters is that Snyder loves controversy and, when none exists, he creates one. Another reason, perhaps, is that Snyder holds himself up to his readers as Bishop Snyder, Founder of The First Church of Blackjack. Many traditional blackjack players need a guru to look up to, and Snyder provides them with this bait.

As I studied his back issues prior to writing this review, I came to the conclusion that most of his readers would rather read about blackjack, write about blackjack and talk about blackjack than actually play blackjack. I have suggested to Snyder many times that he survey his readers and find out how many play blackjack in a casino as opposed to on a computer. He has not accepted this advice as this book goes to press.

To its credit *Blackjack Forum* does publish some useful information. Examples: reports on blackjack games in foreign locations, reports of cheating in blackjack games offered by patrons in bars in Phoenix, and a report by a high roller telling the story of how his money was stolen by a prostitute in Las Vegas.

My main critique of Snyder's *Blackjack Forum* is that he is publishing data about a game that no longer exists. And he is very critical of any system or method that does not meet his defined or accepted criteria of what the game is. Yet his criteria are based on computer-played blackjack, not real-world blackjack.

If you are one of Snyder's readers, accept this challenge: The next time you are in a blackjack game and have lost two or three straight hands increasing your bet into a rising count each hand, tally up how many times you lose that next hand (assuming the count continues rising or stays the same). Or tally up how many times you can walk up to an open table and play heads-up against the dealer and win. Or watch the effect of a "strip shuffle" on a winning game (a strip shuffle is when the dealer picks small segments of cards from top to bottom, reversing their order and creating, in many instances, a choppy game). Then you will begin to get some idea of why I differ with Snyder and what today's game is all about.

• **Blackjack Monthly** by Robert Gates: 12 issues at $60 per year. Richard Canfield & Associates, Escondido, CA.

A monthly evaluation of blackjack games in Las Vegas, Reno/Tahoe and Atlantic City. The evaluation criterion is the number of decks in the game and decks (cards) dealt before the shuffle. This is called "penetration" by traditional blackjack players. The newsletter includes some blackjack tips (e.g., "tell" of the month), a classified-ad section and a schedule of tournaments. The newsletter includes a feature article about a topic the editor considers interesting. The publisher of this newsletter is listed as Richard Canfield & Associates. I would really like to see more input from Canfield if he is, in fact, the publisher. This newsletter is written by a traditional blackjack player for traditional blackjack players and contains nothing of interest to new-era players. The editor does not recognize the existence of table biases caused by the non-random shuffle.

• **Current Blackjack News** by Stanford Wong: 12 issues at $95 per year. Pi Yee Press, La Jolla, CA.

This publication periodically surveys every casino in Nevada and Atlantic City and reports the number of blackjack tables in each casino, number of decks, rules of play, betting minimums and maximums and other data of this type.

The only advantage to the new-era player for getting this kind of data is every so often a casino will come up with an extremely favorable rule upon which knowledgeable players can capitalize. A good example is what occurred at the Silver City casino in 1989. Early surrender (surrendering your first two cards and giving up half your bet before the dealer checks for blackjack) was instituted. This is the most favorable of blackjack rules and gives the basic-strategy player an advantage of 0.25 to 0.5% right off the top of the new deck(s).

However, favorable rules changes like this occur only rarely, so the subscriber is getting, for the most part, a monthly tabulation of table counts, decks used, deck penetration and rules of play for various locations. Of interest only to traditional card counters.

• **The Experts Blackjack Newsletter** by Gambling Times Incorporated: 12 issues at $60 per year. Gambling Times, Inc., Van Nuys CA.

The original idea behind this newsletter was outstanding. Give all the blackjack experts a forum for expressing their ideas and publishing their new methods. It worked great for the first couple of years, with many experts such as Uston, Thorp and Canfield contributing thoughtful and useful articles. But then the articles stopped coming as one editor after the other resigned from the job. The newsletter became a shell of its former self, publishing warmed-over articles from other sources. Stan Roberts, publisher of *WIN* magazine, is now much more active in the editing process and improvement has been noted in recent issues. I am hopeful that this newsletter will make it in its present form, because it is the only one in existence that publishes articles across the entire spectrum of blackjack systems and methods.

Blackjack Learning Aids

I will discuss learning aids under the categories of Schools and Home-Study Courses, Video and Computer-Aided Instruction.

SCHOOLS AND HOME-STUDY COURSES

It is difficult to rate schools in a book because they come and go so fast. Every school rated in the 1980s edition of this book is now out of business except for my own. Schools come and go in various locations, and caveat emptor!

Let me give you a little background on my own involvement in running a blackjack school.

In 1978, with my burgeoning reputation as a blackjack expert, I decided to establish *Jerry Patterson's Blackjack Clinic.* By early 1979 I had trained five instructors, and we were teaching five nights a week in many locations in the greater Philadelphia area. Over one hundred students per month were graduating from my blackjack clinics.

We were teaching recreational gamblers how to play the hands, how to count cards and how to bet according to the count. Our graduates were going out and winning money in the casinos.

It didn't take other blackjack entrepreneurs long to discover this business opportunity, and by 1980, there were more than a dozen blackjack schools open in the Philadelphia/Atlantic City area. Many of them were reviewed in the last edition of this book. None are reviewed herein because all have long since closed or gone on to other locations.

My own instructional activities peaked in 1982 with the establishment of ten Blackjack Clinic franchises. I learned the hard way that blackjack was not a "cookie-cutter" product like some other franchises. I had to support all ten of these franchises—from Florida to California—with on-site presence, and it became too much travel and too much work. So, after assisting the franchises to satisfy their obligations to their students, I disbanded them and went back to what I enjoyed most—playing blackjack, teaching blackjack and developing winning blackjack methods.

There are still many blackjack schools operating in this country besides my own. Most are teaching techniques that at best are hopelessly out-of-date and at worst are losing techniques that will cost you serious money if you use them in the casino. Because these schools are run by local players in remote parts of the country, I don't know who they are and find it difficult to track them because they are not in business very long.

Here is my advice: *Be careful if you attend any blackjack school.* Demand to see the credentials of your instructor. Get student references. And use this book to evaluate what they teach. Is it useful? Are the graduates winning with the school's methods? Does the instructor use the same technique he's teaching you? When was the last time he played blackjack in a casino?

The most important question to ask concerns the school's guarantee. The guarantee should be based on your satisfaction, not your performance over a long period of time. One school operating in the Northeast requires its students to complete lengthy and complicated practice and casino records and submit them prior to considering a refund. The refund should be under your control and with no questions asked.

You have learned in this book that card counting does not always work and must be used only under the proper conditions. But many schools do not tell you this; they are teaching you a technique that is out-of-date except under defined conditions.

When the casinos began changing their shuffles and washes in 1982 to counteract shuffle-trackers, card counting became much less effective; I continued teaching it, but only as one of many winning techniques under the umbrella of my winning TARGET 21 Method.

If you are concerned about any school or are considering entering a local school, send me a copy of their sales brochure and I'll be happy to evaluate it for you. My address is in the back of this book. In doing this, you will be helping other blackjack players because I will make this information available through my blackjack newsletters.

It is interesting to speculate on the demise of the blackjack schools. Why are there so few left? The major reason, in my opinion, is that you cannot teach a recreational or occasional player how to deal with a 1–1.5% long-run advantage over the casino by using card-counting techniques. This 1–1.5% advantage, with the statistical fluctuations in the game, is still the same as gambling to the recreational player; he is told he has a mathematical advantage over the casino but is not told that mistakes easily wipe this out.

Most recreational players do not have the patience to sit in a shoe game and wait for high-count betting opportunities. And when they get these opportunities, they don't understand why they often lose. It's like a jar with 52 white balls and 48 black balls. When you reach into the jar, it's very easy to pull out a black ball even though they are outnumbered. The same goes for losing on high-count situations even in a game with little or no like-card clumping.

Another important point to make regarding blackjack instruction concerns mail-order systems. Many of these systems, marketed by hucksters and fast-buck artists, were evaluated in the first edition of this book. Most were worthless and were identified as such. The majority of the outfits that sold this trash are now out of business because the public has smartened up. I like to think that I contributed to this process.

There are only two Blackjack home-study courses in existence that I am aware of: my own TARGET 21 Home-Study Course and Bobby Singer's Home-Study Course.

The TARGET 21 Home-Study Course is unique in that it features in-casino instruction, periodic update seminars, telephone consultation and access to a blackjack hotline in addition to the Home-Study Package, which includes both video- and audio-based instruction. There is no direct marketing program for this course; it is available only to readers of my books who contact me requesting information. The course costs $295. For further information see Chapter 22.

Bobby Singer's Course is traditional basic-strategy, card-counting and money-management instruction in an audio-based format. It is marketed on certain cable channels by Bobby Singer himself and sells for prices ranging up to $100.

If you buy any blackjack home-study course, make sure it comes with a guarantee and face-to-face interaction with the author.

Video and Computer-Aided Instruction

The casinos themselves seem to be leading the way into the video instructional area. For example, Harrah's Marina in Atlantic City serves as the backdrop for John Patrick's *So You Wanna Be a Gambler! Advanced Blackjack: Card Counting* video tutorial, which is offered for $29.95.

The video contains seventeen errors in basic strategy as well as instruction in an antiquated ten-count system. This apparently has Harrah's licking their chops in anticipation of all the would-be counters flocking to their casino. They'll welcome you with open arms and even buy you dinner!

In my opinion, the only good advice on this tape is Patrick's suggestion that you chart the dealer for a number of rounds before entering the game to see if the dealer is on a "hot trend" or a "cold trend" (although he doesn't spell out exactly what constitutes a hot trend or a cold trend). I also like his advice to leave the table after losing four consecutive hands.

In the arena of computer-aided instruction, there is one major deficiency in the marketplace. Most of the software has been developed strictly for IBM PCs. It's as if Apple or Commodore or the others don't exist. If you own an IBM PC, there is an excellent program by John Imming aimed at the traditional card counter. Its called *Real World Practice Casino.* If you don't own an IBM, the only software available that I can find is called *The Blackjack Tutor*—a program I sponsored a number of years ago and market to readers of my books who request information.

Any computer program that you consider should allow you to specify the number of decks, the number of players in the game, the shuffle point and the rules of play, including peek or no peek under a 10 or an ace. It should also allow you to specify the point-count system by assigning values to each card type. The program should indicate basic strategy errors and keep a running count in the point-count system you have specified. You should be able to check your mental count against the running count at any time.

The program should also allow you to bet with your card-counting strategy, check your bet against this strategy and against a defined maximum bet that depends on your bankroll.

The two programs that meet these criteria are John Imming's *Real World Practice Casino (RWC)* and *The Blackjack Tutor.*

The *RWC* requires an IBM PC, or compatible, with at least 256K or RAM, and a DOS of 2.1 or higher. The program comes on either a $5\frac{1}{4}''$ or $3\frac{1}{2}''$ disc and costs $79. This program contains a couple of nice features, one of which Imming calls a "real-world shuffle." You can specify the type of shuffle and even ask the computer to display the decks during the shuffle. This isn't really a real-world shuffle, but it's nice to have something other than the typical random-number generator set up your decks. The program also allows you to specify when fresh decks are introduced into the game. The other interesting feature is that you can specify a face-up or face-down game.

The advantages of *The Blackjack Tutor* are its availability for many different types of personal computers and, in most cases, the basic configurations of these personal computers. The program has all of the characteristics listed above and sells for $49.95. A disadvantage is the random-number-generator shuffle.

Consultation/Advice From Blackjack Experts

Beware of bad advice! And beware of so-called blackjack experts who offer to play for you and take a share of the profits.

Blackjack and gambling advice are proliferating, from books and newsletters to live and taped video shows. During the 1990s you will be inundated with more advice from "experts" than you will ever need or know how to use. Here is how to separate the good from the bad and useless.

Demand that the teacher or advisor be a player and a user of his or her own advice. Demand to see credentials or watch him in action before you get too excited about following his advice. Any Joe or Jane Schmoe can learn how to talk about these games. But few can put their own advice to work in the real world of casino play. Most of these people make their money by pedaling products, not playing.

Demand to know whether or not your "advisor" has a casino background. Most advisors who have worked in casinos take a casino perspective of the games. For example, ask any pit boss if you should insure a blackjack (a bet offered when the dealer has an ace showing; you are paid 2 to 1 if he has a 10 or face card in the hole) and you will get a yes 99% of the time. This is the pat house answer because this is the way they have been trained, even though this advice is usually not in the player's best interests.

Let's take John Patrick as a specific example. John has a casino background and dispenses advice like this: "If you have any question at the table, any question at all, just ask the dealer. They'll help you out. Remember, they're not your enemy. You're your own worst enemy. The reason you lose at gambling is because you're a dope. You don't know how to play."

Patrick dispenses this kind of advice on his videotapes and on a casino-sponsored cable TV show. He recommends splitting a pair of 5s against a dealer 6 up-card, and he says that you don't know how to play?!

The very worst kind of consultation you can get is the offer to bankroll a "blackjack expert" to a session of play and then split the profits from the session with him or her.

One of my players had this happen before becoming my student. She needed money fast because of a personal problem and borrowed $5000. Somehow she got my number and called me from Las Vegas and described her plans. She was going to hire "Mr. X" (I promised her I would not disclose his name), the author of a blackjack book, to play for her and triple the $5000 loan. (He was going to win $10,000 and split this with her.)

I begged her not to do it, but she was desperate and wouldn't listen. The ending is even more sad than her loss of the $5000. The "expert" was playing in a single-deck game at Caesars, Las Vegas, and getting clobbered hand after hand. She begged him to leave the table but he wouldn't. He, she and the $5000 went down in flames at the one table.

There was no reason for this loss and no reason that anyone should ever accept this kind of offer. Think of how incongruous this is. If a player is an expert, he should have built a large bankroll by now. So why in the world does he need your money to play? I'll tell you why. Because he's a loser. This story will eventually have a happy ending; the woman has learned the TARGET 21 Method and has recouped a portion of her $5000 loss.

THE GAMBLER'S BOOK CLUB

The original gamblers bookstore is The Gambler's Book Club, in business now for twenty-six years. GBC is the prime source of all of your gambling-related material. If any of the books reviewed herein are not available at your local bookstore, you can easily get a copy at GBC. Their free twenty-eight-page catalog lists over 1000 different books on gambling. The store, a landmark in Las Vegas and located at 630 South 11th Street (right off Charleston Blvd.), is open from 9 to 5 daily except Sunday. It is worth an hour of your time on any trip to Las Vegas to stop in and browse. Call them at 1-800-634-6243 for a catalog.

PART THREE

Winning Strategies for Today's Player

11

How to Create and Manage a Blackjack Bankroll

Part III contains four winning strategies for casino blackjack. Before I teach you these strategies, however, it is necessary for you to learn the fundamentals of money management in this chapter and the essentials of mental preparation in the next.

The advice in this chapter is suitable for both the new-era player, who plays for the short-term and exploits table biases caused by the non-random shuffle, and the long-term player, who accepts the premise of random-number-generated card-counting systems.

CREATING YOUR BANKROLL

Most gamblers have no concept of what a bankroll is. When they go to the casino they grab whatever spare money they can get their hands on and hope for the best. If they go with $100 or $200 and lose the entire amount (which happens most of the time), they "create" another bankroll, the next time they decided to visit the casino, by grabbing more money they cannot afford to lose. They keep no records and have no idea how much they have lost over their last few trips, during the last month or the last year. For a number of reasons this is the wrong way to go. An important step on your road to becoming a winner is to treat your bankroll with respect. But first things first. The first step is to define a bankroll, the second is to show how to create one.

Let's first discuss what a bankroll is not. It is not money you can get with a credit card. It is not money you have coming to you such as an income-tax refund. It is not what you intend to save over the next few weeks. It is not money you have in the bank or in a savings account. And, except under certain circumstances which will be discussed below, it is not casino credit.

A bankroll is cold, hard cash you have put together for the purpose of gambling. It is kept separate from your other monies; separate from monies you use for living expenses or monies you have set aside for investment purposes. You should keep your bankroll in a safe place. I suggest, depending on size, you keep it in a safe at home or a safe deposit box at the bank.

Now if you don't like handling and carrying cash, I suggest the following: Open a line of credit with the casino for a minimum amount. This amount should depend on your financial circumstances, for example $500. When you go to the casino, write a marker for the $500. This is your bankroll. When you leave to go home and have won money, be sure to buy the marker back. If you have lost and have less than the $500 left at the end of your trip, the $500 marker will either be treated as a check and sent to your bank for collection or you will be sent a bill for the amount. Treat your credit line with respect and don't be tempted to increase the line to an amount with which you are not comfortable. I would suggest that the amount be no more than 2% of your annual salary. If you are making $25,000, that would equal a line of credit of $500; $50,000 would equal a credit line of $1000; and so on.

TERMS YOU SHOULD KNOW

Now that we have defined a bankroll, let's define the related terms: *betting unit, session bankroll, stop-loss* and *stop-win*. Make a note of these terms, especially betting unit, because we will be referring to them in subsequent chapters.

A *betting unit* is your minimum bet, the bet you start with when you enter a game. It can be $1, $2, $5, $10, $25 or higher. Divide your bankroll by 100 or 200 to get your betting unit. For a bankroll of $500, your betting unit is $500/100 = $5. For a bankroll of $1000 your betting unit is $1000/100 or $10. If you are conservative and want to bet less aggressively, use 200 as your divisor. For example, $1000 divided by 200 is a $5 betting unit.

A *session bankroll* is defined as 20%, or one-fifth, of your bankroll. If you are playing with a bankroll of $1000, your session bankroll is $1000 divided by 5, or $200. This amount is also your session *stop-loss.* If you lose the $200, you terminate the session. I recommend limiting your gambling-session duration to no more than two hours; anything more and you may start to lose control. At the end of a session, or if you drop a session bankroll, take a break for at least an hour. Go out and take a walk on the Boardwalk, have a cup of coffee or take in a bar show. This advice is crucial because it keeps you in control. If you lose your session bankroll and immediately go into your pocket for extra money, who's in control? You or the casino?

What is your table stop-loss? It is 3-6 betting units and, in no case, more than one-third of your session bankroll. Get up and leave the table immediately when this stop-loss is touched. Find another table. Some tables are simply "cold."

What is your *stop-win?* Let's also discuss this in terms of a *session stop-win* and a *trip stop-win.* Your session stop-win is equal to your session bankroll. If your session bankroll is $200, this amount is your winning goal during the session. More conservative gamblers can shoot for 50% of session bankroll; it's up to you. The important idea is to set a goal and stick to it. When you win this amount, terminate your session, take a break and enjoy your win. There is one exception to this rule: If you are in a hot table and winning, stay until it cools off. How do you know when it cools off? When you have given back **no more than** one-third of your winnings. If you are up $300, for example, leave with at least $200 profits in hand.

I realize that many gamblers can't raise more than $100 or $200 for their initial bankrolls. However, I do advise waiting until your bankroll is at a sufficient level to justify a betting unit with the above rules. Nevertheless, some gamblers will take their shot anyway. Here is the money-management strategy for small-bankroll players:

Divide your bankroll into 50 betting units. A $100 bankroll is fifty $2 units; a $250 bankroll is fifty $5 units.

Divide your 50 units into 10 table bankrolls of 5 units each. Do not deviate from this 5-unit stop-loss per table under any circumstances, even if it means not doubling or splitting pairs. Follow the TAKEDOWN Strategy in Chapter 13.

ENERGY LEVEL—HOW IT AFFECTS YOUR PLAY

You must never, never play when you are tired. This is when you are most likely to lose your self-control. Play when your level of energy is high and when you feel well. Try to stick to the same eating habits as you do at home, consuming similar food at similar times. Be aware of your blood-sugar level. If you have the low-blood-sugar syndrome, called hypoglycemia, you may get tired at certain times of the day because of a lack of food intake. You can monitor your energy level at home before your casino visit to determine if you get these tired periods. Your doctor can advise you on blood-sugar tests to help define and solve the problem with proper diet and eating habits.

Be very, very careful with your alcohol consumption. Too much alcohol is the easiest way to lose your self-control. If you've had a few cocktails with dinner and feel like you can win the house, do me and yourself a favor and take just one session bankroll with you and give the rest to your spouse or a friend or leave it in a safe deposit box. All casinos have them.

DISASTER: WHAT TO DO IF YOU LOSE YOUR SELF-CONTROL AND DROP THE ENTIRE BANKROLL

You've come to town on Friday evening for the weekend with a $1000 bankroll. By Saturday evening you've had five disastrous sessions and dropped it all. What do you do? If you drove in, run for your car and head for home. If you are waiting for a bus or a plane, find a way to pass the time without rolling a credit card or signing a marker. Treat yourself to a gourmet dinner and take in a show. Believe me, this will prove cheaper than risking any more of your hard-earned money at the tables. Do *not* go to a restaurant inside the casino. Look in the Yellow Pages and pick a restaurant in town. Don't leave yourself open to temptation.

On Sunday morning take a bicycle ride on the Boardwalk if you're in Atlantic City (8 A.M. to 10 A.M. bikes are allowed). If you are in Las Vegas, drive up to Boulder Dam or better yet take a ride to Valley of the Fire (about a forty-five minute drive, beautiful country and well worth your time). There are plenty of places to stop and look and to hike if you are so inclined. I guarantee you will love the Valley of the Fire. Most visitors to Las Vegas never give it a thought, because it interferes with their action. But you have to take time to smell the roses. And practice your self-control.

If you are in Reno, drive to "the Lake" (Lake Tahoe). Or drive to Virginia City. The old mining town reeks of history and interesting sights.

If you can survive this kind of gambling disaster and make a positive experience out of it, you will look forward to your next trip with the knowledge that you possess the self-control to become a winner.

And be sure to read and follow the advice in the next chapter!

SHOULD YOU TIP THE DEALER?

The subject of tipping is an important part of money management. This is because every time you tip you either reduce your win or increase your loss. Let me teach you how to let the casinos pay for your tips and maximize the tips you give the dealer.

Make a bet for the dealer but don't put the bet in front of the betting circle on the blackjack table. If you do this, the dealer controls the money, not you. Put the dealer's bet on top of your own. Announce this to the dealer: "You're riding along with me on this hand." If you lose the bet, that's the end of it. The dealer has lost too. But he or she knows that you made the bet because you announced it.

Now if you win, you have one of two choices. Let's say you bet $1 for the dealer. Put it on top of your bet as defined in the prior paragraph. Assume you win the bet. You can immediately give the $1 won to the dealer after the payoff and leave the original $1 you bet up for the next hand.

Or you can bet the dollar you just won for the dealer on the next hand and let the dealer control that bet while you leave the original $1 bet on top of your bet for the next hand. I prefer the latter because it gives the dealer a chance to win $2 instead of $1.

The casino forces the dealers to take their bets down after each hand. Why? Because on a hot hand they don't want the dealers profiting along with the gamblers. But when you control the tip money, the dealer rides right along with you. And they really appreciate it. If you don't understand the above discussion, take out some plastic chips and walk through it a few times. It's easy. And it will save you a lot of money. This is because a $1 bet can become $10 or more for the dealer on a series of winning hands. Now you are tipping with money won from the casino, not yours.

CASINO COMPS, RATINGS AND COMP CARDS

A discussion of casino comps in a chapter on money management? Certainly! "Comps" is the jargon for complimentaries or "freebies" given by the casinos to keep the patrons there as long as possible, tempt them into betting more money and encourage them to come back when they leave. I have seen a cup of coffee cost a gambler hundreds of dollars. Why? Because he waited for it. When the pit boss comps you to dinner, it takes him some time to get the approval. In the meantime you may be playing at a losing table. But you wait for the comp. And lose a couple of hundred more. Is it worth it? Of course not! If you are ready to leave the table on a losing streak, leave! Don't wait for the coffee or the comp. If the comp is in the works, check back with the pit boss later. Leave the table and let him know: "I'll check back with you."

In Atlantic City, if you are betting any kind of money (or "action") at all, the pit announces to you that they are "rating" you. All this means is that they watch your action and record your average bet size, total action and win and loss in the computer. They use this data to determine whether or not they will comp you and for how much. But this policy encourages gamblers to play for the house and ignore their own money-management policies. I have seen numerous gamblers play beyond a stop-loss just because they were being rated. This is silly! No, it's more than that; it's stupid! It's OK to be rated, but walk away when you are ready to walk. Don't worry about your rating.

The same advice applies to the comp cards pit personnel hand out in many of the Atlantic City casinos. The purpose of the comp cards is to encourage you to get rated, build up a record of time and action and qualify for comps. This is fine and you should take advantage of the casinos' generosity. But on your terms, not theirs. Leave the table on a table stop-loss and forget about the rating. It can be detrimental to your bankroll.

MONEY CONTROL

When you are in a game you should be aware of how much money you have in front of you. Suppose you buy into a game for $100 and run into a hot table. The dealer is breaking and your winning chips are accumulating on the table. You have $1 chips and $5 chips mixed together and you have no idea how much you actually won. Now the dealer starts winning and you begin to give some of the chips back. If you are not careful, you might lose all the money you just won simply because you don't know how to "control" your money.

Here is the solution. When you are winning, the first thing to do is separate your buy-in from your winnings and place it into a separate stack. Count your winnings when the shoe is being shuffled. Use different-colored chips for stop-win amounts. (For example, use a white $1 chip to segregate $100 of winnings from the rest of your winnings.) You can also put your stop-win (the amount you have "locked up" and will not dip into at this table) in a different spot on the table to separate it from other winnings you are playing with. When you hit a stop-win, leave the table. Money control is extremely important in making these critical decisions and is a key to gaining the winning edge. Practice it!

Because of the importance of money management, let's summarize what you have learned in this chapter.

SUMMARY OF WINNING TIPS AND IDEAS

- Create your bankroll from cash you can afford to lose and store it in a safe place.
- If you prefer not to carry cash, open up a minimum line of credit that equals about 2% of your annual income. Respect your credit line and do not abuse it.
- Define the betting unit for the level of risk you wish to take: to determine your betting unit, divide your bankroll by 200 if you are conservative or 100 if you wish to take more risk. Gamblers with small bankrolls of $250 or less should divide them into 50 betting units.
- Define your session bankroll and your stop-loss for any session as 20% of your casino bankroll. Keep your session duration to two hours or less. If you double your session bankroll, terminate your session, take a break and enjoy your win.
- When you are in a winning streak at one table, give back no more than $\frac{1}{3}$ of the money you have won at this table before leaving the table.
- A table departure is triggered by losing $\frac{1}{3}$ of your session bankroll or a stop-loss of 3-6 units.
- Never play when you are tired.
- Don't be tempted to use credit cards or cash checks if you drop your entire bankroll. Relax and enjoy the local sights.
- Tip the dealer by controlling his or her bet with your bet, rather than by making a separate bet for him or her.
- Don't wait at a losing table for a comp. Come back for it.
- Practice sound money-control principles as defined in this chapter.

MONEY-MANAGEMENT WORKSHEET

My initial bankroll is: _____

The bankroll divisor is: _____

My betting unit is: _____

My session bankroll is: _____

My session stop-loss is: _____

My table stop-loss is: _____

My session stop-win is: _____

Comments and ideas for creating my bankroll:

12

An Easy-to-Use Strategy for Developing and Executing Mental Discipline

BACKGROUND

In my 12+ years of teaching I have never failed to offer instruction on money management in the home-study course or classroom. I taught my students how to establish a bankroll and how to bet in relation to their bankroll. Many of them listened to me, practiced their betting procedure and then went to the casino and did something entirely different. Why? I kept asking myself. I knew what they were doing because they called me up to discuss why they lost. The problems always boiled down to a lack of mental preparation, to the student's inability to operate in a casino environment. Because let's face it: When you walk into a casino they want you to play on their terms, not yours. That's why they bombard you with free drinks, loud music, myriad colors and a free-and-easy atmosphere. That's why you play with chips and not money. After all, what's a chip but a piece of plastic? Most gamblers are mesmerized by the typical casino environment and lose all self-control. If they had any kind of game plan at all, they quickly forget it in the excitement of the action. If they lose, they roll a credit card and get more money.

I began to realize that there was a missing link in my instruction—teaching my students how to exercise self-control and mental discipline. I conducted research activities into the psychology of gambling in conjunction with experts in this field whom I met through my blackjack classes.

The major finding of these research activities is simply this: Mental preparation and self-control are 90% of the game! You can learn the fundamentals of the games and how to bet but if you are not mentally ready to play, your level of risk is just too high.

You've got to realize that many mistakes inside the casinos are the consequence of problems outside the casino. Understanding and dealing with this relationship is very important on your road to becoming a winner.

Think back. How many times have you felt mesmerized and totally out of control, pulling more money out of your pocket without wanting to, staying at tables longer than you knew you should, playing too many tables and losing more than your session stop-loss? These are the problems that you've got to deal with before you can start winning on a consistent basis.

The bottom line is not just how much you take off the table, it is how much you *don't lose,* how much you *don't give away* to the casino. This aspect of your game plan is just as important as your winning tables. How many times has a big win been nullified by unnecessary losses? This is another example of a problem that must be addressed before we get into the technical-skill areas.

Let me give you a framework for preparing mentally for each casino trip and session. Mental preparation consists of following these five steps:

1. Establishing Goals and Objectives
2. Developing and Documenting a Game Plan
3. Practicing Visualization of Goals And Objectives
4. Executing the Plan
5. Monitoring and Evaluating the Plan

STEP 1: ESTABLISH GOALS AND OBJECTIVES

First answer the question: Why am I gambling? For fun? To get away once in a while from a stressful environment? To feel the rush of an adrenaline high? To make money and win on a consistent basis? To make a living? Most people gamble for fun and enjoyment, but others are more serious about the games. After you answer this question you can decide what you want to accomplish; what goals you want to realize.

For example, if you wish to gamble to win on a consistent basis or to make a living, you should choose blackjack as your primary game because you can get an advantage over the casino. If you're gambling for fun, you have to decide whether or not you want the action or the money. For example, if your goal is to double your bankroll on a weekend's play, what do you do if this occurs on Saturday and you still have plenty of time left for action? You need to think about and write down these overall goals and objectives. Many high rollers are happy to break even. They get the thrill and glamour of the casino, everything they want for free, and if they play smart, it doesn't cost them a dime.

Let me suggest a goal to you. Build a bankroll. How much money are you playing with now? $500? $1000? Why not establish a goal of building a gambling bankroll of $5000 or $10,000? Then you can live like a king or queen and let the casinos pick up the tab for all your expenses (which they are perfectly willing to do).

When you think about your goals and begin to write them down, be as specific as possible. For example, let's say your goal is to build a $5000 bankroll. Attach a time frame to this goal. Think about what you will do with the money. Your goal might be expressed as follows: "I plan to build a $5000 bankroll within the next six months and use this money as the down payment on a new car." Or—"I plan to build a $5000 bankroll within six months and use it as a permanent blackjack bankroll that allows me to play as a green chip ($25) bettor."

Here are other goals you can consider for your own play:

- Become a professional player
- Let the casinos pay all your expenses and be treated like a VIP

- Become a consistent winner as a part-time player and supplement your income
- Enjoy the action offered by the casinos—break even and avoid heavy losses
- Travel to exotic places and use blackjack winnings to pay for the trip

But establishing a goal is just the first step. Now you must think through how you intend to accomplish the goal. On to Step 2.

STEP 2: DEVELOP AND DOCUMENT A GAME PLAN

After you've listed your goals, decide how you intend to accomplish them. Think about how often you intend to visit the casinos. Decide how much money will be in your initial bankroll. Buy a spiral-bound notebook and handwrite a page or two. Here is an outline of what to write:

- goals and objectives
- schedule of casino visits
- blackjack methods I intend to master
- mental-preparation process I intend to use
- schedule and drills for home practice
- money-management parameters (review money management—Chapter 11)
- Typical trip plan including trip duration, casinos to play, session schedule

You will be surprised at the satisfaction you derive from the simple exercise of writing these items on a page or two of paper. Okay, you have established some goals and you've thought about and planned out how you're going to achieve these goals. What's next? Step 3! It is based on one of Dr. Steve Heller's techniques called "triggers." Dr. Heller is a well-known Southern California applied psychologist.

STEP 3: VISUALIZE THE ACHIEVEMENT OF GOALS AND OBJECTIVES

If you have ever read a self-improvement book, you will understand what this is all about. You are asked to visualize in your mind what it is you intend to accomplish. And you are asked to do this on a daily basis or even a few times during the day. Many successful people attribute their success to visualization techniques. Properly used, they can help anyone, especially the casino gambler. Here are a few tips to get you started. Visualize an event that can realistically happen. For example, do not visualize winning $100,000 at the blackjack table, because there is very little chance that will occur.

Take a specific goal such as adhering to a stop-loss. Suppose your session stop-loss is $100 and your objective is to take a one-hour break if you hit that stop-loss. In the past you have not done this, but too often played right through your stop-loss. Visualize yourself walking away from the tables and going out onto the Boardwalk or out into the sunshine and taking a walk. You can also do the opposite and visualize yourself stopping after your win goal has been accomplished. Suppose your goal is to win $500 for the weekend. See yourself winning the $500, terminating your gambling activities and enjoying the pool and sunshine for the rest of the weekend. Or visualize the win, getting into your car and driving home. Each visualization should take no more than one minute.

Here is one more tip on doing your visualization exercises. Take one goal, attach a mental picture to it and visualize it at night before you go to bed. Many studies have proven this to be the most effective hour of the day. However, do not visualize more than one goal at this time. You can visualize one goal for a week or two, until you notice some positive results, and then change to another one.

Steve Heller's Triggers Technique is nothing more than a method for reinforcing positive results. If you are doing something right toward accomplishing one of your goals, reinforce it in your subconscious mind so that you can use the good feeling associated with this "win" at a future time when you need it.

Here's how: Suppose, for example, that one of your goals is to leave a table after losing 6 units, something you have had difficulty adhering to in the past. On your next trip to the casino you decide to make a special effort to follow this stop-loss procedure. Your first table turns out badly, but you feel good about leaving after losing 6 units. Pick a spot on your body to touch, say the back of your left hand, and touch that spot as you experience the "good feeling." That is your "trigger" for this goal. Every time you leave a table after losing 6 units, touch this spot. And feel good about it. Feel good about the discipline of adhering to a stop-loss. You are reinforcing a positive action!

Now, how do I use this trigger? you are asking. Here's how.

Suppose you are sitting at a table and are down 5 units. You double down, lose the hand and now you're down 7 units. You decide to play one more hand because the dealer was just lucky on that last hand and should have never beaten you. But wait a minute! Who's in control here? You or the casino? You touch the back of your left hand and reexperience the positive feelings that are associated with the trigger of leaving the table after a stop-loss. You regain control and leave the table.

At this stage we have established our blackjack goals, developed a game plan and visualized the positive outcome of our plan. Now it's time to talk about plan execution, Step 4 of the process.

STEP 4: EXECUTE YOUR GAME PLAN

To execute your game plan, write an agenda much like a travel agent does when he or she schedules a trip, no matter the duration: a day, weekend or a week. Write everything on paper. Be sure to schedule your gambling sessions on a daily basis. Start each day with the time you arise and end with the time you go to bed. List the casinos at which you intend to play, the time you intend to play and the duration of each playing session. Show your lunch and dinner breaks. And add the time you intend to take to "smell the roses."

Remember one of the tips from the last chapter—limit your

gambling sessions to no more than two hours. If you find yourself getting tired, or losing control in any way, don't hesitate to stop before your session time is up. A plan is nothing more than a guideline.

Follow your plan within reason. Obviously, if you are winning heavily at one table, don't leave the table to keep to your schedule. The purpose of the plan is to put you in control of your gambling activities. When you do this once and execute the plan, you will understand the benefits: It will help you to control your emotions. What you want to accomplish with this step is to play according to your schedule and your requirements—not the casinos'.

STEP 5: MONITOR AND EVALUATE THE EXECUTION OF YOUR GAME PLAN

This is a very important step because it allows you to update your plan with ease. This involves keeping a table-by-table record of your casino play. For example, let's say you play a blackjack table. What was your bankroll going into the table? How long did you play? How much did you win or lose? What was your betting unit? **Carry a pocket notebook and document these items immediately after playing each table!** If your goal is to become a winner, you must do this and you must make it a habit. It only takes a few seconds after each table, but the payoffs are great. Now you can evaluate your play in an unemotional, detached manner after each session. You can determine how well you followed your plan and what problems you encountered. **And you can take corrective action!** The satisfaction you will derive from following this simple procedure will amaze you. Do it!

Here is a summary of the items of information that should be documented for each table you play. You can copy them directly to your pocket notebook as column headings:

- Date
- Time of Day
- Casino Name

- $ Win or Loss
- Cumulative $ Win or Loss for This Session
- Play Duration
- Cumulative Play Duration for This Session
- Comments on This Table Such as Mistakes Made or Distractions That Affected Your Play

13

TAKEDOWN: A 4–Phased Non–count Strategy for Today's Player

INTRODUCTION TO THE STRATEGY

If you have ever played blackjack in a casino, you may remember a table at which you could do no wrong, the dealer kept breaking and you won hand after hand. Afterward, you may have wondered, "If only I had known, I would have bet much more aggressively."

This is the chapter you have been waiting for. After reading it you "will know" because it describes a strategy for exploiting a winning table, a table where the non-random shuffle has caused a bias that favors the players. This strategy, called TAKEDOWN (a stock market slang term meaning "take down" a profit or sell and take profits), detects short-term opportunities and shows you how to profit from them.

Here I aim to teach you how to profit from a winning table when you find yourself in one, without counting cards! Many players think that a winning table happens by pure chance, that the dealer's breaking hand after hand and "dumping" money to the players is pure coincidence, that they were just lucky to be in the right place at the right time. Well, this last thought is right. They are lucky to be there when the dealer starts dumping. But winning tables don't always occur by chance. And when your table starts dumping, you should be prepared to take advantage of it. Here's how.

TAKEDOWN is comprised of four phases:

- Phase 1: Table Evaluation
- Phase 2: Buildup
- Phase 3: Score!
- Phase 4: TAKEDOWN

These phases are simple to define. Phase 1 occurs after you enter a game. Using small betting units, you *evaluate* the table for potential. If the game doesn't pass a simple test and meet your conditions, you either depart or continue in the game, not losing or winning much, waiting for the conditions to be met.

Your goal in Phase 2 is to *build up* a substantial win without risking a lot of money. The game has proved itself as player-biased; you are beating the dealer and winning units.

When you enter Phase 3 in this game, you have already locked up a percentage of a hefty win. With the remainder of the win, your goal is to *score*, to win a much larger amount in this game with no risk whatsoever!

When your initial profit goal of Phase 3 is satisfied, you immediately enter Phase 4 and start *"taking down" profits. You will learn to stay in the game with your win-lock increasing as profits accumulate. Once Phase 4 is entered, you are guaranteed a table departure with your pockets bulging with chips.*

Let's get into the details. In the following paragraphs I will teach you how to recognize each phase and how to move from one phase to the next. It important that the goals of each phase be met before ascending to the next.

PHASE 1: TABLE EVALUATION

A mistake that many blackjack players make is buying more chips than they should be prepared to lose at any one table. When you buy in for $100 or even $50 at a $5 table, it is easy to stay until you lose this amount. The average player doesn't have the discipline to leave a table with part of his buy-in still in front of him.

The rule on the buy-in amount is to buy in for a little more than your stop-loss. If your stop-loss is 6 units, *and it shouldn't be more*, buy in for 10 units. This will cover a double or pair split should it occur on your last hand. But be prepared to pick up 4 units and walk should your stop-loss be triggered.

When you enter any blackjack table don't be too quick to raise your bet. Evaluate the table for at least the first 2 to 3 hands. If you win 2 out of 3, with the dealer breaking on at least one of these hands, proceed to Phase 2. If you lose 2 of 3, take it easy. And play to a short stop-loss. Remember, play no more than 6 betting units, preferably a 3-5 betting-unit stop-loss. If you lose 2 of 3 hands followed by a series of alternating wins and losses (a "choppy game") without reaching your stop-loss, you will have to decide whether you want the action of playing the hands or whether to look for another table. If the choppy game continues for 1-2 shoes, I recommend looking for another table. If the choppy pattern breaks, you start to win, and find yourself up 3 betting units, then proceed to Phase 2.

PHASE 2: BUILDUP

Buildup means a gradual increase or expansion. That is the purpose of this phase.

We build up our buy-in amount as the table starts to pay off. The rule for Phase 2 is to win 3 flat bets before raising your bet. A flat bet is betting the same amount on each hand. For example, betting $5 a hand, your goal is to win 3 of these $5 bets, or $15, before raising your bet according to the rules discussed below. Important point: It will usually take you more than 3 hands to win the 3 bets; I am not suggesting that you win 3 bets in succession. Using the same $5-a-hand betting example, if you play 6 hands and win 4 hands, you have won 2 bets, or $10 ($20 for the 4 hands won −$10 for the 2 hands lost = $10 total win). You have not yet realized your objective, $15. If you play 7 hands and win 5 ($25), clearly you are ahead 3 bets (assuming no double downs or blackjacks). You have won $25 on your winning hands and lost $10 on your losing hands; you are up $15; your goal accomplished, you now proceed to the next betting level.

A betting level is defined as a specific number of betting units. Level 1 requires you to bet one unit. In the above example, our bet size was a one-unit bet of $5.

Betting level 2 requires you to bet 2 units, or $10 (I will continue to use $5 as a sample betting unit; you can substitute whatever your own betting unit is that you have defined from Chapter 11).

The TAKEDOWN Method consists of five betting levels: a one-unit bet at level 1; a 2-unit bet at level 2; a 3-unit bet at level 3; a 4-unit bet at level 4 and a 5-unit bet at level 5.

Obviously, you are increasing your bet by one unit at each level. Your goal at each betting level is to win three bets, or $15, at level 1; $30 at level 2; $45 at level 3; $60 at level 4 and $75 at level 5.

You must ascend through these five betting levels before you proceed to Phase 3.

Chart 6 summarizes this betting strategy and also shows you your stop-loss for each betting level. Remember—your goal at each betting level is to win three bets. Notice I said *bets*, not *betting units*. As defined above, your bet increases by one unit at each level. To review once again: Your bet size starts at $5 (or one unit). You flat-bet until you are ahead three bets and then increase your bet size by one unit through each betting level. The reason for this increase is because the game or player bias is getting stronger and stronger.

A series of three losing hands will abort this betting pattern. The chart shows your bet reduction on each of the three hands. If your stop-loss is triggered, you either leave the game (preferably) or revert to Phase 1 and start over.

The only question not answered in this table is what to do after you reduce your bet on a loss and then you win the next hand, i.e., bet $10, lose; bet $5, win. The answer is, you increase your bet by one unit back up to the size associated with this level. For example, you're in level 4 and betting 4 units or $20. You lose; you bet $15 on the next hand. You win; you bet $20 on the next hand. You lose; you bet $15 on the next hand. You lose again; you bet $10 on the next hand. You win; you bet $15 on the next hand. You win again; you bet $20 on the next hand. Now you stay at $20 until you have

CHART 6: TAKEDOWN
PHASE 2 BETTING STRATEGY

Betting Level	Bet Size No. of $5 Units	Win Goal 3 Bets	Stop Loss	Betting Sequence On Series Of Losing Hands		
1	1 ($5)	$15	$15	5	5	5
2	2 ($10)	$30	$20	10	5	5
3	3 ($15)	$45	$30	15	10	5
4	4 ($20)	$60	$45	20	15	10
5	5 ($25)	$75	$60	25	20	15

won your 3 units and then move to level 5; five betting units, or $25.

The above example shows the one weakness in this method—a choppy table. If you chop back and forth, you're winning the smaller bet and losing the bigger one. This is where you must respect your stop-loss and depart the table or revert to Phase 1.

Notice that when you complete the five levels you have won a total of $225, or 45 betting units. Now don't get too excited and rush out to play this system, because you won't accomplish all five levels that often. You will abort the pattern many times long before you get to level 5. But you will abort with a profit if you leave the table; if you stay, you may give some of your winnings back. Notice that your stop-loss at each level never returns all your winnings to the casino; you always abort with a nice profit.

Question: Do you count a doubled win or loss, or a pair-split win or loss, as two wins or losses in totaling your three wins or three losses for each betting level? I suggest a conservative approach: Total a win as winning only one bet, but total a loss as a loss of two bets. In this way you will exit a game with your doubled profits in hand while not risking any more money at each betting level.

To summarize Phase 2: Ascend five betting levels and win 45 betting units.

On those few occasions—and they will occur in strong, player-biased or dealer-breaking games—when you do reach the pinnacle at the end of the fifth level, you will have built up a nice little bankroll of 45 units starting with a buy-in of ten units and a stop-loss of 6 units (as defined in Phase 1). Not bad. But this is just for starters. Now we go to Phase 3!

PHASE 3: SCORE!

If you get this far, you are probably playing at a dealer-breaking table. Or you are playing at a very strong player-biased game. So get ready to play much more aggressively, but with just a fraction of your win: 20 units ($100). Put your buy-in amount plus the other 25 units in your pocket as a win-lock, that is money which is not to be touched in this game under any circumstances!

Using a "Fibonacci Series" (see below), you are going to bet up on each win if certain conditions are met.

Leonardo Fibonacci lived in the middle ages and attained the distinction of becoming one of the most eminent mathematicians of his time. His greatest contribution to the world of numbers was the so called "Fibonacci Sequence." This series of numbers (1, 2, 3, 5, 8, 13, etc.) came into existence through a recreational problem having to do with the production of a pair of rabbits over the course of a year. Most modern-day numbers crunchers are familiar with this scholar's work, including certain stock-market forecasters who employ the "Elliot Wave Theory" to predict movement in the stock market. Some forecasters believe that some natural cycles that occur in the universe can be predicted to follow a Fibonacci pattern and are thus predictable.

For our purposes we will use the sequence to determine our next bet size depending on the outcome of the hand, whether or not the dealer breaks and whether the hand was a double down or split-pairs hand.

Here are the rules:

First, notice that each number in the Fibonacci Sequence is computed by adding together the prior two numbers. Three is 1 + 2. Five is 2 + 3. Eight is 5 + 3. Thirteen is 8 + 5. And so forth. The series looks like this if extended out a few more terms: 1, 2, 3, 5, 8, 13, 21, 34, 55, 89, 144, 233, etc. For betting purposes, we express each of these numbers in units. Again using $5 as our betting unit, we bet one unit or $5 to start.

On a win and a dealer break, we proceed to the next number in the Fibonacci Sequence and bet that in units: 2 units, or $10. Again on a win and a dealer break, we move up the sequence and bet 3 units, or $15. Now the betting becomes more aggressive as we move up to a 5-unit bet ($25), an 8-unit bet ($40) and so forth.

If you get to Phase 3 in the TAKEDOWN Strategy, you are playing at a dealer-breaking table or "Home Run" table: a table exploding with profits, a dumping table. (I have heard some pit bosses refer to these tables as dump trucks.) Use the Fibonacci Sequence and bet aggressively to exploit this very exciting situation.

By this time your adrenaline will be pumping wildly; be sure not to let this interfere with computing the correct-sized bet and following the specific betting conditions set forth below.

- Start with a one-unit bet ($5). If you win the hand and the dealer breaks, move to the next number in the sequence for your next bet. Or, if you win and the dealer does not break, bet the same amount. A double-down or split-pair win would override the dealer non-breaking hand and allow you to move to the next number in the Fibonacci Sequence, i.e., you win a double-down hand, the dealer does not break, OK to move to the next number in the sequence.
- If you lose a hand, you move back two levels to get your next bet size, i.e., lose betting 21 units; next hand bet 8 units. If you lose two hands in succession, revert to a one-unit bet. Or, if your bet is above 3 units and you lose a double down or pair-split hand, you revert to a one-unit bet.

After starting with 20 of the 45 units you won in Phase 2, your initial goal in Phase 3 is to win at least 15 additional units. As soon as this is accomplished, you enter Phase 4. If you lose the 20 units, leave the table.

Question: When getting into the higher betting levels of the

Fibonacci Sequence, should I ever consider deviating from the basic strategy for playing the hands and not risk the additional units called for by a double down or pair split? Yes, because the loss of a doubled hand can be devastating psychologically. Also, a loss can wipe out most or all of the profit won at lower levels. A safe rule is to double down or split pairs only if the dealer shows a low card (2-6), a potential breaking hand, but then if and only if you won the last hand. Remember, you are executing a short-term strategy and you are not obligated to follow a basic playing strategy that is based on long-run mathematics. (For a description of the basic strategy, refer to Chapter 20.)

PHASE 4: TAKEDOWN

Now you are looking to "take down" your profits and exit the table.

There is a very simple rule for table departure. This rule is great common sense; it is not original. I first read about it in one of Huey Mahl's columns in *The High Roller Sports Newsletter*. It is simply this: Do not give back more than one-third of your profits. So, if you are 15 units ahead, your stop-loss is fixed at 5 units. (Remember, you don't enter Phase 4 until you are at least 15 units ahead.)

Suppose you win another 8 units for a total of 23 ahead. Move your stop-loss up to 7 or 8 units.

This stop-loss money-control method is very easy to follow at the table. Simply divide your winnings from Phase 3 into three piles of chips. Keep the three piles equal sized. That is, as you win money, divide the chips equally among the three piles. After accomplishing your 15-unit win goal in Phase 3, your three piles start at five chips each. As you continue to win, the three piles grow in equal proportion, six chips per pile, seven chips per pile, and so forth.

Now suppose you go into a losing streak. Work off one pile, only not touching the other two. When that pile is gone, you're gone; it's as simple as that. If you start winning again, build this pile up until it equals the size of the other two. Then they all start growing at the same rate again.

Question: Can you dip into one of the other two piles if you need chips to double down or split pairs as called for by basic strategy? No! Don't do it. Respect your win-lock. Remember, we are playing a short-term game. We are protecting our win at this table right now. We are not playing for the long run. Do not accept the axiom of the traditional player that says you must play basic strategy on each and every hand.

Final Question: I can already hear my aggressive readers thinking, "Why do I have to ascend through all five betting levels of Phase 2? Why not just ascend through three levels and then proceed to Phase 3, especially if the dealer is breaking frequently?" OK, I'll give you three levels but not two! And if you're conservative, stick with all five. You'll leave more tables with a profit.

PRACTICE FOR TAKEDOWN STRATEGY

You can practice computing the correct bet size and determining your stop-losses and stop-wins by having a spouse or friend deal you winning hands at home. The idea here is for your "dealer" to deal from six decks of cards, but deal with the cards face-up and "set up" your winning hands. Not every hand should be a win; instruct your dealer to deal you two winning hands out of three. I suggest practicing your Phase 2 bets, ascending through the five betting levels, locking up your 25 units (or more) and then practicing your Phase 3 bets with the 20-unit bankroll won in Phase 2. Practice setting up your three-chip piles and entering Phase 4 as soon as you win 15 units in Phase 3.

CONCLUSION

In a typical weekend's play you will not find many tables that will take you through all four phases of the TAKEDOWN Strategy. You may not even find one. But . . . you will reap profits as you ascend through the betting levels of Phase 2, even if you depart the table on a stop-loss at any one of these five levels. And . . . when you do find the Home-Run table, you will be ready to exploit it for sure!

I have promised to teach traditional card counters how to take advantage of the non-random shuffle and exploit the realities of today's game. I will keep that promise in Chapter 15 after teaching you in Chapter 14 how to count cards and how to use the count.

14

A Handbook of Card-Counting Drills

INTRODUCTION AND DEFINITIONS

This is a transition chapter between the non-count strategy called TAKEDOWN described in Chapter 13 and the three-card counting strategies described in the next chapter. Before you can understand, learn and implement these three strategies, you must learn how to count and how to use the count.

In this chapter I will teach you how to count in both hand-held and shoe games and in games where the cards are dealt face-up or face-down. Card counting is easy and, if you can add 1 + 1 and get 2, you should have no problem in developing this skill. Eleven copyrighted drills, from a Card-Counting Home-Study Course I once sold for $295, are included to make learning easy and fun.

A brief lesson on card counting was included in Chapter 2, and I will pick up from where that lesson left off. You are starting off the top of a fresh deck or shoe with a count of zero and subtracting one for each face card, 10 or ace you see, adding one for each 2, 3, 4, 5, or 6 that you see and ignoring all neutral cards: 7, 8, 9. This is called the "running count" because it runs right through the deck or shoe, from top to bottom. Earlier in this book I defined the True Count as the running count divided by the number of decks left to play. (Note: Learning Drill 10 in this chapter teaches how to estimate the number of decks left to play.)

The True Count is more aptly defined as a "count per deck." To understand what this means, assume you have a running count of 12 with 3 decks left to play. Twelve divided by 3 yields a True Count or count per deck of 4. The count per deck of 4 means that you have about 4 extra high-cards distributed in each of the 3 decks left to play—a more accurate depiction of the value of those high cards. To be consistent, I will continue to use the term True Count to define this simple calculation. (How to bet with the True Count is explained later in this chapter).

To conclude this chapter, I will instruct you how to use the True Count for betting purposes. Many advanced card-counting strategies use the True Count to play the hand, but this is too difficult to learn and totally unnecessary in today's blackjack environment.

LEARNING DRILL 1: CARD FAMILIARIZATION

The purpose of this exercise is to familiarize you with the values of the cards: Low cards are 2-6 and equal + 1; neutral cards 7-9 and equal zero; high cards are 10s, face cards and aces and equal −1.

Take a deck of cards and turn over one card at a time. Announce the value either out loud or silently as you prefer. When you turn over a low card say, "Mi 1"; a high card is just "1" with no prefix; and a neutral card is zero.

This is not a *counting* drill. Do the exercise until you are completely comfortable in recognizing the value of each card.

LEARNING DRILL 2: SINGLE-CARD DECK COUNTDOWN

This is done the same as Drill 1 except you now keep a running count as you flip over the cards. Your count should start with zero and end with zero since since the 20 high cards (−1) balance out the 20 low cards (+1) and, of course, the neutral cards count zero. As you count down the deck, think the count silently to yourself. When you see a neutral card, just repeat the count for the last card. And remember to use the prefix "mi" for all minus counts.

Since you are counting down a balanced deck equal to zero, you should know the value of the 52nd card before you flip it over. For example if your count is "mi 1," the last card must be a low card (+1) to bring the deck back to zero.

If you make a mistake with this last card, you have made an error. Do not shuffle! Count down the deck again and get the zero count.

Practice this drill until you can count as fast as you can turn over the cards—about thirty seconds for the entire deck.

LEARNING DRILL 3: TWO-CARD
PATTERN-RECOGNITION DRILL

You will quickly learn that it is easier to count cards if you recognize the 6 two-card combinations: the "mi 2" combination is any two high cards; the "mi 1" combination is one high and one neutral card; the zero combination is a high-low pair or any two neutral cards; the +1 combination is a low and a neutral card; and the +2 combination is any two low cards.

To learn these combinations, take a deck of cards and, instead of turning over one card at a time as in Drill 1, turn over two cards at a time and announce their value. Go through the entire deck, announcing each two-card combination as you flip it over. Remember, this is a familiarization exercise so do not keep a running count.

Do this drill until you are completely comfortable with each two-card combination. It will prepare you to count in any blackjack game.

LEARNING DRILL 4: TWO-CARD DECK
COUNTDOWN

This drill is the same as Drill 2 except you are turning over two cards at a time instead of one. Start at the top with zero and keep a running count through the deck. Pause before turning over the last two-card combination. You should be able to accurately predict its value. If not, do not shuffle, and count down the same deck once again.

Initially, strive for accuracy and not speed. That will come with Drill 5.

LEARNING DRILL 5: DECK SCAN

After you master the first four drills, you may want to improve your card-counting speed. This drill is similar to Drills 2 and 4 except that you hold the deck in your hand and scan cards instead of turning cards over from the top of the face-down deck. Hold the deck in your left hand, face-up, and push cards from left to right off the top of the deck.

Initially, keep the count in two-card combinations as in Drill 4. As you become more adept, you will scan 3-, 4- and even 5-card combinations.

With a little practice you will scan a deck in twenty seconds or even less. Do not try to break the world's record of nine seconds! There are better things to do with your time.

You can also do this drill by breaking a shuffled six-deck stack into about six piles. The size should be easy for you to pick up and scan. Set these six piles in front of you. Starting with the pile on the left, pick up each pile in turn and scan from left to right, scanning from the top of the pile to the bottom (reverse if you are left-handed). Carry your count from pile to pile until you finish. Your count should be zero. At the beginning of this drill you can set aside 2-3 cards. At the end of the drill you should be able to tell the count of the set-aside cards. For example, if your count at the completion of the scan is +3, your three cards set aside should be three high cards (−1, −1, −1) to bring your count back to zero.

In the beginning, your target for completing this drill is two minutes. If your goal is to become a serious card-counter, you should be able to scan six decks in 1:20 or less. I have seen professional players break one minute with this drill. My personal best is 1:09.

LEARNING DRILL 6: MULTI-CARD HAND DRILL

The purpose of this drill is to teach you to maintain the running count while making a hitting decision in a multi-card hand (a hand with three or more cards). Multi-card hands often present problems for neophyte card-counters.

To start, use two decks of cards to make up a special training deck composed of 25 low cards, 8 aces and 6 neutral cards (put the other cards aside for the next drill). Shuffle up this special deck and deal yourself hands. In each hand, deal cards until you get a soft 19 (a hand totaling 19 with one ace counting as 11) or better, or hard 17 (a hand with all aces counting as 1) or better. With the 25 low cards, you will find that most hands will contain three cards or more.

As you deal the cards, total the value of your hand, make your hitting/standing decision and keep an accurate running count. At the end of each hand, set it aside for later review.

When you reach the end of your training deck, the count should be +17 (25 low cards minus the 8 aces are +17). If you have made an error, recount the hands that were played.

LEARNING DRILL 7: MINUS-COUNT DRILL

Many neophyte players have difficulty in counting on the minus side of the scale. This drill is to correct that difficulty.

Take the cards left over from Drill 6 and shuffle them thoroughly. These cards have a value of −17 (as the cards used for Drill 6 were +17, the leftovers must equal −17 to balance the two decks to zero).

With this special deck, do a single-card countdown similar to Drill 3. Because of the unbalanced deck, most of your running count values will be on the minus side of the scale.

After you are comfortable in counting down the deck, practice keeping the count by dealing out three hands. Draw cards to each hand until it is 17 or better. Keep a running count through all three hands. When you finish dealing to a set of three hands, push them aside and deal three more. Continue until you are finished with the deck, shuffle and repeat the drill.

LEARNING DRILL 8: FACE-UP BLACKJACK GAME DRILL

In Atlantic City games where the dealer's first card is dealt face-up, start your count with this card and move clockwise around the table after the second card has been dealt to each player. You count the two-card combinations of which there are five: (1) two high cards are counted as −2, (2) one high card and one neutral card are counted as −1, (3) a high card and a low card or two neutral cards are counted as zero, (4) a low card and a neutral card are counted as +1, (5) and two low cards are counted as +2.

From this point on you count each card as it is dealt, including the dealer's hand. You carry this count forward from hand to hand until the end of the shoe, at which point you start over from zero.

The Face-up Game Drill is the practice routine for developing the skills necessary to count down the six-deck game. Deal out hands from a six-deck stack. Play the hands with perfect basic strategy. Keep a running count as you deal and play. Use chips and play one of the hands as your own. Make a bet with the True Count (see page 37) or according to the Non-Count strategy in Chapter 13.

This drill develops mental alertness and concentration. You are performing five activities simultaneously: dealing, playing the hands, keeping the count, computing the True Count and making a betting decision. If you have trouble with the drill, approach it in a gradient fashion. Start by dealing and playing the hands. Then add the count when you feel comfortable with this gradient. The True Count and bet can come last.

LEARNING DRILL 9: FACE-DOWN BLACKJACK GAME DRILL

The counting procedure in a face-down game is quite different, and more difficult, than in the face-up game. You start by counting the dealer's up-card and then your hand. As the other players hit their hands, these cards are dealt face-up; count them as you see them. If a player breaks (his hand total exceeds 21), he tosses his first two cards (those dealt face-down) face-up on the table. While the dealer verifies the break, you count these two cards. Any player wishing to double down or split pairs must turn over his two unexposed cards. Count these as they are turned. After all the players play their hands, count the dealer's cards as they are drawn, after counting the hole card. Then, as the dealer settles each bet with those players still in the game, he turns over each player's two unexposed cards so they lie on the table nearest the dealer. Count these cards as the dealer flips them over; remember, the two uncounted cards are always nearest the dealer.

You now have an updated count from this hand. Here is the drill for practicing this face-down card-counting procedure.

On a tabletop and with six decks of cards, deal out four player hands, face-down, and a dealer's hand, first card down, last card up. Deal the hands so that the dealer's is on top of your little practice semicircle and one hand, your own, is directly in front of you on the table.

Starting your running count with zero, count the dealer's up-card and then count your two cards.

Without looking at the other hands, deal them cards at random, face-up. You are simulating the play of these other players' hands. You don't care whether these hands are played correctly or not; this is for your counting experience. Count each of these cards as it is dealt, just as you would in a real game.

Now play out the dealer's hand, counting each card as it is dealt.

At this point you simulate the settlement of bets by turning over each player's two unexposed cards, placing them face-up and positioned nearest the dealer's hand. Count them as you turn them over.

Push the cards from this hand aside and repeat this process, dealing out hands, until you reach the end of the six decks. Check your count against the remaining cards to make sure you get the zero count.

LEARNING DRILL 10: REMAINING DECK ESTIMATION DRILL

Knowing the number of decks remaining to be dealt is requir-ed to compute an accurate True Count and for other reasons you will learn in the next chapter. Here is how to compute this number.

Purchase 30 decks of Bee brand playing cards. With 23 of the decks create the stacks as shown below and tie them with rubber bands:

- Stack 1: 4½ decks
- Stack 2: 4 decks
- Stack 3: 3½ decks
- Stack 4: 3 decks
- Stack 5: 2½ decks
- Stack 6: 2 decks
- Stack 7: 1½ decks
- Stack 8: 1 deck
- Stack 9: ½ deck

These are your models; learn to recognize the size of each of them. Now take six decks from the remaining 7½ and practice cutting stacks that equal the size of your models. Visualize the cards you cut as remaining in the discard tray. As you cut each stack and compare it with the appropriate model, mentally subtract the number from the number of decks in the game to compute remaining decks. For example, if you cut a two-deck stack and there are six decks in the game, subtract 2 from 6 to compute remaining decks. If you cut a 3½-deck stack and there are eight decks in the game, subtract the 3½ from 8 to get 4½ remain-ing decks.

Do this drill until you are skilled in estimating decks played and remaining decks to the nearest quarter deck (13 cards). If your normal practice session is one hour, you should devote 5 to 10 minutes to this drill.

LEARNING DRILL 11: TRUE-COUNT COMPUTATION DRILL

There is an easier method for computing the True Count than dividing running count by remaining decks. Instead of dividing by remaining decks, you multiply by the inverse of remaining decks. For example, if there are $5\frac{1}{2}$ decks remaining in an 8-deck game, you divide the running count by $5\frac{1}{2}$ to compute True Count. An easier method is to multiply by 0.2 (1 divided by $5\frac{1}{2}$). Assume that 14 is your running count. Now think of 14 divided by $5\frac{1}{2}$. Did you get the number right away? Look how much easier it is to multiply 14 times 2 and get 2.8 (the 2 is really 0.2; you can add the decimal point afterward).

Here are the multipliers all worked out for you. For this drill memorize and practice the multipliers for the game you are playing. For instance, if you are playing mainly 4-deck games, memorize the values of $3\frac{1}{2}$ down to one decks. Use this table to add the computation of the True Count to the deck estimating that you do in Drill 10. Here are your multipliers for the one-deck game:

HOW TO BET WITH THE COUNT

Once you have learned to compute a True Count, betting with the count is easy. Just bet the True Count in units. For instance, if your betting unit is $10 (see Chapter 11 for how to compute betting units), and the True Count is 4, your bet is 4 times $10 or $40. Do not bet more than 6 units on any one hand.

HOW TO PLAY YOUR HAND WITH THE COUNT

Unless you are a semiprofessional or professional player with two exceptions, you should not waste your time learning complicated strategies for varying the basic strategy with the count.

For the majority of blackjack players, the only two hands in which you should use the count to vary your play are (1) player 16 vs. a

Remaining Decks	Multiplier
7.5	0.15
7.0	0.15
6.5	0.15
6.0	0.15
5.5	0.2
5.0	0.2
4.5	0.2
4.0	0.25
3.5	0.3
3.0	0.3
2.5	0.4
2.0	0.5
1.5	0.7
1.0	1.0

Here are your multipliers for the one-deck game:

Cards Played	Multiplier
13	1.3
17	1.5
26	2.0
33	3.0
39	4.0

dealer up-card of 10 and (2) any player hand vs. a dealer up-card of ace—the insurance decision.

The decision for 16 vs. 10 is simple: If the running count is any minus, hit your hand. If the running count is any plus, stand. If the running count is exactly zero, you can flip a coin—it really doesn't matter. This hand occurs quite frequently and, if you learn how to count, you should learn how to make this play.

The second decision—taking insurance—is a little more complicated. (See page 219 for a complete description of insurance.) On the insurance decision, you are betting that the dealer has a blackjack, that he has a 10-value card in the hole. This is a good bet if the True Count is equal to or greater than 3, and if you are not playing into a low-card clump.

If you are playing into a low-card clump, the running count will have increased very rapidly, for example from $+6$ to $+11$ in a 4-player game. A simple rule for determining whether or not you are in a low-card clump is to remember how the running count increased over two successive hands. If the running count increases by more than the number of players in the game in each of the two hands, you may be in a low-card clump; do not take insurance.

Taking insurance in a face-down game is much more difficult because of the unseen cards.

When you take insurance in a face-down game, you need all the information you can get, right then, in the second or two that you have to make the decision. The problem is that you might have a very high running count or True Count, sufficient to take insurance, but there are many unseen cards on the table that will influence your count. You must adjust your count for as many of these unseen cards as you possibly can. Here's how.

First, observe the cards of the players' hands on either side of you. Adjust your running count accordingly. Now comes the hard part: you must deduce the other players' unseen cards.

If another player has tucked his two cards under his chips, that means he is standing and probably has a pat hand. Assume the count of this hand as -1. If a player takes insurance on a pat hand, you can assume he has a 20 and assign a count of -2. If the a player is holding his two cards in his hand, you can assume he either has a stiff hand or a hitting hand and assign a count of zero. If a player insures this type of hand, he is probably holding 10 or 11 and you can assign a value of $+1$. All of these deductions must be made very quickly and totaled up into your "temporary" running count. If this running count is 2 or higher in a single-deck, go ahead and take insurance. In the face-down shoe game, the running count must meet the conditions described in this paragraph.

After you finish this "temporary count" for insurance purposes, revert to the "real running count" by eliminating your "deduced counts" and counting the cards as they are seen.

Now that you have been exposed to the basics of card counting, you are ready to tackle the three new winning strategies in the next chapter. I shouldn't say new, because these strategies are based on my thirty-four years of playing experience. But they are new in the sense that, to my knowledge, the strategies, with one exception, have not been published elsewhere. A simpler version of **Playing on the Run** was published in *Gambling Times on Blackjack*.

15

Strategies and Tactics for Card Counters

BACKGROUND DISCUSSION

In this chapter I will teach you three new card-counting strategies. While allowing you to capture your mathematical advantage over the house, they still recognize the realities of today's game as discussed in this book. You will learn in this chapter that each of the three strategies has been designed for certain game conditions. The bad news is that you have to scout for these game conditions (I will show you how in this chapter). The good news is that once you find them, you have a lesser chance of losing and a much higher chance of winning.

One of these three strategies, the *Count Reversal System,* protects you from the devastating effects of like-card clumping. Here's a little background on that problem.

Nancy talks to hundreds of card counters every year. They call our blackjack school looking for help and for ways of turning losing sessions into winning ones. Would you like to know their most significant problem, the one that also seems to be the most common among these counters? It's simply this: They lose when betting up into rapidly rising counts. If you have read this book carefully, you will know why this happens: When the count is increasing, low cards are being dealt. Low cards favor the dealer because he will break less often. The dealer, of course, plays his hand last and, even if he does break, does not return your money if you break first.

There is an easy solution to this problem. Do not bet up into rapidly rising counts. In fact, do not raise your bet until the count reverses and begins a *downward* trend. This is not easy for the traditional card counter to accept. But it works. Do it. In this chapter you will learn a **Count Reversal Strategy** that will provide you with two major advantages: (1) You will lose less and maybe even win in games with like-card clumping; (2) You will win in games you heretofore may never have played—games that exploit the like-card-clumping phenomenon.

But, before describing Count Reversal and the other two strategies, it is important for you to learn an important fact about card counting and how this fact may affect your game. In shoe games (the majority of games are shoe) high-count betting opportunities occur less than 5% of the time. Card counting is a waiting game that many new players do not understand, waiting for high-count betting opportunities to occur.

Another problem often occurs in conjunction with infrequent high-count betting opportunities.

For example, picture yourself at the blackjack table in a shoe game. You are making one-unit bets and playing two or three shoes without a high count. This happens quite frequently. You're getting bored when all of a sudden it happens. Two or three hands with a plethora of low cards and the count takes off. Plus 7. Plus 10 with five decks left to play. Your adrenaline is pumping and you push the money out there. You lose. The count continues to advance. Plus 16 with four decks left to play. I can't lose this hand, you think, as you push out a 4-unit bet. You draw a 17; the dealer draws a 20. The count is now +20. You push out a 5-unit bet. You draw a 10 to the dealer's 6. I've got him now, you think, as you push out another 5 units for the double down. You draw a 4 for your double card. Oh well, you think, he's going to break this hand. The dealer turns over a 4 for a total of 10, and your heart sinks as you wait for the inevitable 10. But wait. He draws a 3; your adrenaline pumps again as you wait for the breaking card. It doesn't come. The dealer draws a 6 for a standing total of 19 and beats you once again.

Recognize the scenario? It happens all the time. What do you do on the next hand as the count goes to +22? Increase your bet once again? Don't do it! Playing my Count Reversal Strategy protects you from these kinds of losing scenarios. You would have bet only one unit on each of the above hands as you wait for the count to reverse and the high cards to start appearing.

But there is yet another problem with this scenario that you should recognize before we can make some progress. It's psychological and concerns the 5% statistic for high-count betting opportunities. You are getting bored making your one-unit bets on about 19 out of 20 hands. You are hungry for action. So when a high-count betting opportunity does occur, you plunge in and seize the opportunity, giving in to your adrenaline high.

This is a natural thing to do for most gamblers, but you must recognize it as a problem if you want to become a consistent winner. You have to decide whether you want a higher chance of winning or whether you want the high-count betting action. It's a decision we all have to make and should be recognized as such.

The three winning strategies described below are designed to solve these problems and to provide you with the best chance of winning money.

WINNING STRATEGY 1: PLAYING ON THE RUN

If you are a card counter and sincerely want to win, you must recognize that the old strategies no longer work; you must prepare yourself, mentally, to adopt a new strategy. **Playing on the Run** works for the face-up shoe game. It replaces two out-of-date strategies that I recommend you reject:

First, unless you are playing the TAKEDOWN Strategy described in Chapter 13, *reject the strategy of locking yourself into one table.* There are two problems with this strategy.

1. Because of like-card clumping, you may never get any high-count betting opportunities.

2. You are wasting time waiting for high-count betting opportunities to occur. If you still insist on walking up to any old table and

sitting down to play, walk away if you haven't won 3 units within the first seven hands or by no later than the end of the first full shoe. If you stay, use TAKEDOWN.

The second strategy you must reject is *back-counting*. Back-counting is standing in back of the table, behind the players, keeping a count without entering the game, and waiting for the count to reach a level associated with a mathematical advantage over the dealer. The first problem with back-counting is too much exposure, especially in the Nevada casinos. You will be marked very quickly by the pit bosses as a card counter and they will watch you like a hawk. The second problem with back-counting is that it takes too much time. You may back-count half a shoe and never get a high enough count to justify table entry.

OK. If you're not going to commit to a table, and you are not going to back-count, just what is left? you may be thinking.

Playing on the run.

To employ this technique, you must learn to walk by a table, scan the cards and quickly pick up the count. If the running count is equal to or greater than the number of decks in the game, you have a table-entry signal. Mathematically you have an even game. The only variable here is the number of decks in the game. Most shoe games in Nevada are six decks; most in Atlantic City are eight decks. The exceptions to this rule can be determined by noticing the size of the discard tray—the short ones are for four decks.

If you sweep an entire casino without finding one playable game, there may be a reason. Do not waste too much time in this casino. Give it one more sweep, looking for the plus count equal to or greater than the number of decks in the game. This plus count should be on the table as you walk by.

If you do not find a playable game in this second sweep, leave the casino and go to the next one on your list.

How to Handle the Discard Tray When Playing on the Run

When you enter the game, make a bet equal to the True Count in units. This will usually be one unit because, remember, all you are looking at prior to table entry is one round of play, one hand by each of the players. Handle the remaining decks as though it's the beginning of a shoe and you are playing off the top. Remember the level of cards in the discard tray (the number of decks already dealt) so you can compute the True Count by counting remaining decks from this point on. Mentally, you are placing all the cards in the discard tray behind the cut card. You haven't seen the cards. You don't know what is behind the cut card. It's the same as starting from a fresh shoe except, of course, your cut card is placed farther toward the front of the shoe. That is why it is safer but not mandatory to use this technique near the top of the shoe. If you jump in at the middle of the shoe, you are essentially playing in a game with a four- or five-deck cut card. This cuts down on your overall advantage for that shoe, but still enhances your overall game and your profits because you are playing more efficiently. Remember, the trick is to assume that all the discards are behind the cut card and you're starting at base zero. And remember your base in the discard tray, the number of decks already dealt and stacked up there when you enter the game.

How to Bet When Playing on the Run

After you make your first bet, which is equal to the True Count in units, do not automatically increase your bet with the count. Only bet the True Count after a winning bet. After a losing bet either bet the same amount (aggressive bettors) or revert to one unit (conservative bettors).

If the count decreases to less than the number of decks left to play, you no longer have a mathematical advantage. But do not let this fact encourage you to leave the table. Stay in the game as long as the count is descending. If you are winning on a descending count, you have two alternatives for determining your bet size: (1) bet the same as your last bet; or (2) increase your bet by one unit with each successive win. Continue betting with your chosen alternative until the count reverses, until you lose, or until the end of the shoe—whichever comes first. Then leave the game and look for another one.

Tips for Playing on the Run

To become adept at this strategy you must practice a table-scan drill at home. Have a spouse or friend deal hands on the kitchen table. When they are finished, take a quick look and time yourself on how fast you pick up the count. You flunk if your count is off, even by 1. Shoot for 10 seconds initially, with an ultimate goal of 5 seconds or less.

In many casinos there are mirrors located above the tables. The pit personnel use them to help monitor the action at the tables in their pit. You can use them, too, for your table scan. In Resorts Casino in Atlantic City you can scan five or six tables in seconds by using these mirrors.

If you are tall like me, you can scan across the pit at the tables on the other side. You need good eyes to do this, but it does save time. If you see very little "paint" (high cards) on a table across the pit, you'd best rush over there to pick up the plus count.

This strategy is easily worked by miniteams or partners. Assume you visit the casinos with one or two of your friends. The three of you deploy yourselves across the casino. Now, when you are scouting, look for one of your friends already at the table. Enter the game with confidence because you know you have the high plus-count.

But you must work out a signaling method for your friend to signal you the count. Red and white chips can be used for this purpose. So can positions on the arm, beginning with the wrist and working up the side of the arm for various values of the count. In Atlantic City, where there is no fear of barring, you can communicate verbally as long as you don't make a habit of it in any one pit or casino.

Playing on the Run delivers another, extremely important advantage: it finds games in which the Count Reversal Strategy can be employed. You will learn how Playing on the Run becomes a transition to the Count Reversal Strategy in the next section.

WINNING STRATEGY 2: THE COUNT REVERSAL STRATEGY FOR BEATING THE SHOE GAME

The theory of this strategy is completely opposite to traditional card-counting theory. Traditional theory says bet up into a rising count. This strategy does the opposite—it calls for betting up into a decreasing count and holding your bet constant on a rising count. If you have read prior chapters carefully, the approach should make some sense even if you don't totally agree with it. Remember that on a rapidly rising count, more low cards are being dealt. Low cards favor the dealer because he breaks less often and players don't win their double downs. Therefore do not raise your bet until the count reverses and the high cards begin to appear. High cards favor the player because of $1\frac{1}{2}$-to-1 payoffs on blackjacks (the dealer's chances of drawing a blackjack are the same, but he does not collect the $1\frac{1}{2}$-to-1 bonus), more wins on double down and pair-split hands, and the dealer breaking more often on stiff hands.

This strategy works best in games with clumping that produces high counts. Many of the shuffles in the Atlantic City and Las Vegas casinos engender these kinds of shoe games. This strategy does not work in choppy games.

It is recognized that in many shoes you will find a choppy count-pattern; increasing and decreasing on successive hands and staying in the neutral zone. For example, a count bouncing up and down on every hand: from $+5$ to $+1$ to -3 to $+3$ to $+7$ to $+5$ to $+6$, and so on is a choppy game. Our research has shown that this pattern may persist over several shoes. If you find yourself in a choppy game, and you are not winning, leave the table and find another game.

The Count Reversal Strategy works well in the huge casinos of Atlantic City. Many of the so-called blackjack authorities berate the Atlantic City casinos, saying that it is no longer possible to win there. This is because they don't know how. There are over 800 blackjack tables along the Atlantic City Boardwalk's linear mile. If you don't find a table in one casino, you can easily walk out the door, onto the Boardwalk, and to the next one just a short walk away.

Here is a tip for scouting for tables in which to employ the Count

Reversal Strategy while playing On the Run. You should saunter at a comfortable pace through the casino with your eyes on each successive blackjack table. Watch for one where the dealer has just finished shuffling and is putting the decks back into the shoe, or better yet, a table with the first hand already dealt. And then scan the table and pick up your count. If the count is heavily negative, keep walking. You are looking for a plus count, but on this first hand a zero or even a count of −1 to −3 might keep you there pending the outcome of the next hand.

If you see a dealer just starting to shuffle, make a mental note of the table location and continue scouting in the general vicinity. If you find nothing better, come back to this table and wait for the first hand to be dealt.

Execute this scouting strategy while playing On the Run. With a little practice, you will find it quite easy to scout for tables simultaneously that meet the criteria of both strategies.

Executing the Count Reversal Strategy

Here is how the Count Reversal Strategy works:

1. Look for a shoe game where the shuffle is just finishing, where you can play off the top of a fresh shoe.

2. Back-count the first two to three rounds. You are looking for a plus count after the first two or three rounds of play. If your count is minus 4 or lower, leave the table and look for another game.

3. What you want to see at this point is the count continue to ascend in round after round. Do not be tempted to enter the game on this high-count situation. You are looking at a low-card clump. Remember, the objective of counting is to find a deck rich in high cards. But these high cards must be dealt for you to realize an advantage. In this game they are still hiding farther back in the shoe. Hopefully, they will begin to appear before the cut card, signaling the end of the shoe, is dealt. But you must wait and see. To enter these kinds of games is to enter a game where the dealer has the edge.

4. Ideally you would like to see the count ascend to twice or even 3 or 4 times the remaining decks left to play. If three decks have

been dealt out of a six-deck shoe, you would like to see the count ascend to +9 or even +12. If you get a count reversal in the +8 range, this is OK but not as much of an advantage as the higher numbers.

5. When the count is equal to twice the number of remaining decks or higher, you begin to look for a count reversal. Wait for a count reversal before entering the game. For example, with three decks left to play, if the count is +6 or higher at the end of this round and then decreases to +3 at the end of the next round (3 less than the count at the end of the last round), this is your table-entry signal.

6. Now you must compute your bet size. Divide the count by the number of remaining decks to get a True Count and make a bet in units equal to half the True Count. For example if your entry count is +12 and there are three decks left to play, bet 2 units for your first hand (True Count is 4). But in no case bet more than 3 units on this first hand.

7. This first hand is key to whether or not you stay in this game. If the count continues to descend, you stay in the game with a rigid stop-loss strategy. Here is your betting strategy for this first hand:

- If you win and the count descends, increase your bet by 50%, i.e., if you bet 2 units, increase to 3 on the next hand.
- If you lose and the count descends, make the same bet on the next hand.
- If you win and the count increases once again, give it one more chance to reverse but cut your bet in half. You don't want to get caught in a choppy game; this is why you reduce your bet.
- If you lose and the count increases, reduce your bet to one unit for the next hand.

8. The general strategy from this point on is to stay in the game as long as the count is descending or as long as you are winning. A descending count means that the high cards are coming out and you have the advantage. But this doesn't guarantee a win; no game is worth playing if you can't beat the dealer. Set your stop loss at 6 units and leave at once if the stop-loss is triggered.

9. After the first two hands, if you win on any ascending count, cut your bet down for the next hand and depart if the count continues to increase after this next round of play. If you lose on any ascending count, reduce your bet to one unit for the next hand. Depart the table if the count increases for two hands in succession. If you win on any descending count, increase your bet by one unit on the win. Do not, however, bet more than 5 units on any one hand.

10. Our primary goal is to get out of this game with a win. This means that once you are up 6 or more units, you lock up half and play with the rest. If you lose these 3, you have hit a stop-win. Take your win-lock money and leave the table. Playing with 3 units means that you reduce your bet to one unit and go from there as before. The apparent conflict between this rule and rule 9 is resolved by never betting 5 units until after you have locked up 3 units after a win of 6.

11. Playing with a stop-win strategy also means the basic strategy is modified if necessary to protect your win. Never dip into win-lock money to double down or split pairs. There is no law that says you have to follow basic strategy. Your short-term win is more important than doubling or splitting on this hand and jeopardizing your table winnings.

12. Continue your betting strategy even if the count dips below zero! You are playing into a high-card clump; the high cards are coming out and you have an advantage regardless of the count. So continue with your betting strategy until the count reverses. Then depart.

13. If you depart on a win and you are near the end of the shoe, you can stick around and count down the next shoe to look for another table-entry signal. Many shoes come right back after the shuffle with the same card-distribution pattern as the prior shoe. Be careful of using this tactic, though, in any Nevada casino; the pit boss may recognize your playing pattern as that of a card counter. In Atlantic City, where regulations prohibit barring, you can use this tactic without any worries.

14. If you pick up a count of minus on the first hand dealt off the top of a new shoe and a continued minus on the second and third hand, you are playing into a favorable 10-card clump, and here is how

to handle it. Enter after the second hand, if your count is equal to or greater than the number of decks in the game but on the minus side., i.e., −7 in a six-deck game. And bet just the one unit. To stay in the game you must get a win and a continuation of the minus trend. For example, your −7 should now be −8 or lower after your first hand. Leave at the first reversal or after the second loss in succession after winning the first hand.

Again, the Count Reversal Strategy goes against traditional card-counting theory, which tells you to bet up into a rapidly rising count. This is wrong and you jeopardize your bankroll every time you do it. Why bet up into a low-card clump when the dealer has the advantage? Sure, you are betting that the high cards will come out on the next round, but I call this gambling; I don't necessarily have the edge on this next hand. I want some proof that the large cards are really coming out and not stuck behind the cut card before I increase my bet.

Traditional theory also says reduce your bet when the count goes down. This is also wrong because these hands indicate exactly when you do have an edge—the high cards are coming out! Go for it!

An Example of the Count Reversal Strategy in Action

Here is an example of the Count Reversal Strategy in action. Let's assume that you are in a eight-deck game with three players, have back-counted the first three rounds, and have a count of +5.

Round 4: +9 with $1\frac{1}{2}$ decks dealt out

Round 5: +10 with $1\frac{3}{4}$ decks dealt out

Round 6: +12 with $2\frac{1}{4}$ decks dealt out

Round 7: +14 with $2\frac{3}{4}$ decks dealt out

Round 8: +11 with 3 decks dealt out (Count Reversal)

Enter the table and proceed to Step 6 of the method. Compute a True Count by dividing +11 by 5, yielding about 2 and rounding to a bet of one unit. (The numbers below for each step correspond to the numbers in the description of the strategy.)

Step 7: You win the hand and the count drops to +9. You bet 2 units.

Step 8: You win the 2-unit bet and the count drops to +6. You bet 3 units.

Step 9: You win the 3-unit bet but the count goes up to +8. You are now up a total of 6 units. You lock up 3 and play with the remaining 3.

Step 10: With your 3-unit table bankroll after the win-lock, you bet one unit. You lose the one unit with the count descending to −4.

Step 12: You bet one unit into the negative count. You lose as the count continues down to −8. Continue playing until you hit your stop-loss or until your new win reaches 6 units. At this point you exercise your win-lock strategy once again, locking up another 3 units for a total win-lock of 6 units.

An Alternative Betting Method for Traditional Players

If you have difficulty accepting the new ideas in this chapter, I suggest testing them at home by dealing out 20 shoes and evaluating the results. Keep track of your betting both ways: by betting with the count on all hands regardless of the direction and by betting with the Count Reversal Strategy. Keep a score sheet of bets for each hand: a column for a traditional bet with the count and a column for a bet determined with the Count Reversal Strategy. This should convince you of the validity of the strategy. You can set up a special training shoe by stocking the first half with extra low-cards and shuffling each half separately.

But if it doesn't, and you still cannot accept the idea of waiting for a count reversal before raising your bet, how about waiting for a win to trigger a bet increase? And how about flat-betting on a win when the count is decreasing on the way down? If you win on the way up, parley your bet or bet the True Count in units. If you win on the way down, do not decrease your bet to whatever the count calls for, but bet the same amount as the prior hand. This betting pattern is also a very effective tactic for fooling the pit bosses. They will not suspect that you are counting.

AN OPTION FOR ACTION PLAYERS

But I came to play, you say. I'm not interested in walking around
looking for tables with many low cards showing. I want to select a
table, sit down and just play. There is an easy solution. Watch for
a count-reversal opportunity at your table. Be alert off the top of each
new shoe. When the count takes off, hold back. Don't raise your bet
until you observe the reversal. Use the betting rules in the Alternative Betting Method for Traditional Players.

WINNING STRATEGY 3: HIGH-LOW-PLUS—A STRATEGY FOR BEATING THE SINGLE-DECK GAMES

Traditional card-counting methods work best in single-deck games.
This is because, since there are only 52 cards in play, the game is
more predictable. However, there are still biases in the single-deck
game that work in favor of either the player or the dealer. **High-Low-
Plus** is based on the realities of today's game and delivers more than
a mathematical edge to the astute player.

It will keep you in games in which you are winning; it gets you
out of games in which you are losing. In winning games, High-Low-
Plus maximizes your win and minimizes your loss. What more could
you ask of a strategy?

First of all, find a game where three, four or more rounds are dealt
per deck before the shuffle. This means that you should limit your
games to those with two or fewer other players. Ideally, including
yourself, there should be no more than three hands dealt per round
of play (not including the dealer's).

The basic concept involves determining your bet size, after the
shuffle and at the start of the new game, by how you did in the last
deck, whether you won or lost. Then you use the count to determine
your bet size for your subsequent second and third hand of each
deck.

In general, if you are winning, you increase your bet at the start of each game; if you are losing, keep it the same, reduce it or depart the table.

Rules for Determining How Much You Bet After the Shuffle at the Start of Each New Game

- Win 2 of 3 hands or 3 of 4 hands in prior deck: Increase bet by one unit (for first game upon table entry, bet one unit);
- Neither win nor lose in prior deck: bet same as last deck;
- Win 1 of 3 or fewer hands in last deck, i.e., any loss in last deck: reduce bet by 50% for first loss; reduce to one unit after second loss. Remember, here we are talking about a loss in the last deck, over 3 to 4 hands, not the loss of one hand.

The above rules are for the "plus" part of the High-Low-Plus Strategy. Next I will discuss the rules for the "High-Low" portion of the strategy.

How to Use the High-Low Count to Make the Betting Decision

As discussed previously, the High-Low Count involves assigning $+1$ to cards 2-6; 0 to 7,8,9; and -1 to all 10s, face cards and aces. You keep a running count as each card is seen.

Here are the rules for using the count to decide how much to bet on your second and subsequent hand of each deck:

- Win last hand and plus count: Parley your bet, i.e., let everything ride;
- Win last hand and minus count: Increase your bet by 50%, i.e., bet $10 on last hand, then bet $15 on this hand;
- Lose last hand and plus count: Bet same amount as last hand;
- Lose last hand and minus count: Reduce bet by 50% or bet just one unit.

Other Rules

Your buy-in amount is 10 units. Your stop-loss is 3-6 units.

A conservative stop-win strategy is to lock up 5 units every time you win 10 units and play until you lose the other 5 units. Example: Buy-in for 10 units. Win 10 units. Lock up buy-in amount plus 5-unit win, or 15 units. Play with other 5 units until they are lost or until you win 5 more units. Each time your playing units equal 10, lock up 5 units and start over.

An aggressive stop-win strategy is, if you have won 20 units or more, continue playing until you give back no more than $\frac{1}{3}$ of your total win. Keep your total win in three equal-sized stacks. Use one stack as your betting stack, and when that stack is gone, depart. If your betting stack grows larger than your other two stacks, be sure to keep the three stacks level by moving chips to the other two stacks. Every time you move chips in this manner, you are locking up money.

SUMMARY AND CONCLUSIONS

In this chapter I have described a basic card-counting strategy for playing the shoe games: *On the Run.* I have showed you how to scout for tables that meet the criteria for the *Count Reversal Strategy* while playing On the Run. And I have included a counting strategy, *High-Low-Plus,* for playing the single-deck games found in many Nevada casinos. All of these strategies recognize the realities of today's game. Learn how and when to use each one and you will win; you will experience the joys of getting in, getting the money—and getting out!

Let's put it all together in the next chapter: **A Seven-Step Winning Program.**

16

Summary—Putting It All Together—A Seven-Step Winning Program

I have thrown a lot of data at you in this book. Systems and methods in Part I. Books, newsletters and other blackjack information sources in Part II. More systems and methods in this Part III. If you've read this far, you are serious about the game and possess the desire to become a winner. Let me now focus your winning energy and show you the seven steps you must follow to become a permanent and consistent winner at casino blackjack.

STEP 1: DEVELOP A WINNING ATTITUDE

Believing you can win doesn't mean that you will automatically go to the winning tables and be dealt winning hands. What it does mean is that you will play on *your* terms and not the casinos. You will play when your level of energy is highest and you can control your emotions. You can develop a winning attitude by practicing the visualization ideas or by using Dr. Steve Heller's "Triggers Tactic" discussed in Chapter 12. Whatever approach you take, stick with it because it will pay off; not only by increasing your winnings but also and, more importantly, by decreasing your losses. Players with winning attitudes know *when* to play—and when *not* to play.

STEP 2: SELECT A WINNING METHOD

This is a key decision and you should give it your utmost attention. Reading this book and becoming familiar with the strategies and tactics presented will help you to make this decision. One suggestion: Do not get caught up in the vortex of evaluating card-counting point-count systems. I evaluated eleven of these in the first edition of this book, and there have been at least that many more published in the last decade. My conclusion is the same now as it was then: If you count or decide to learn how to count, use the *High-Low System*. Higher-level point-count systems look good on paper, but they break down under the realities of casino play.

You should think of your card-counting method as only one of a number of tools that you need to win. Remember, this tool applies to only 5% of the hands that you play at the blackjack table.

Here's how to start. If you are a card counter, or decide to become one, learn one or more of the three card-counting strategies described in Chapter 15. When you get tired of scouting for games that meet the criteria required by these two methods, play the non-count strategy in Chapter 13 at your chosen table while you wait for high-count betting opportunities to occur.

Another important tool you need is a method for evaluating table biases. Or, at the very least, the recognition that they exist and must be dealt with. I have given you some data in this book to start you out. To learn more about table biases and how to use the 18 factors of the TARGET method for selecting winning tables, consider acquiring the TARGET/Blackjack Home-Study Course described in Chapter 22.

STEP 3: JOIN A SUPPORT GROUP; GET INVOLVED WITH A NETWORK OF WINNERS

Let me give you one of the secrets of becoming a consistent winner. Associate with winners. Get to know winners. Hang around with winners. Their winning attitudes will rub off on you. And you will talk to them, watch them play, practice with them and find out how they do it. Avoid losers.

You can develop your own support group by getting involved with your friends that play blackjack. Or by teaching them how to play and what winning is all about.

If you are a high roller with a line of credit, the casino may provide your transportation to and from the casino. If they fly you to Atlantic City from New York, for example, you will meet many other gamblers like yourself. Get to know them on the plane and keep an eye on them in the casino. It will be easy to separate the winners from the losers. Associate with the winners and form your support group this way.

What does a support group do? Members exchange information with each other about systems and methods. They talk over problems about why they might have experienced a losing session. They read and discuss the same blackjack books. (But be sure to read the ones recommended in this book.) Support-group participants arrange for joint-practice sessions and schedule joint trips to the casino. Some even form teams and pool bankrolls or teams to acquire and exchange information about the location of good blackjack tables on the casino floor.

An easy way to get involved with a support group is take my Home-Study Course or attend one of my classes. I don't teach that much anymore, just once a year in major gambling locations, but blackjack players who attend my classes form friendships and support groups that last the rest of their lives. My blackjack Home-Study Course involves periodic update sessions that provide the opportunity to meet and get involved with other players. And forming support groups is one of the major functions of **The Casino Gamblers' Network** tm discussed in Chapter 22.

STEP 4: DEVELOP A PLAN OF ACTION

It is always surprising to me why so few gamblers develop and document a plan for their blackjack training and their blackjack play. In their careers and everyday business world, they would not think of operating without a plan. Presidents of major corporations have attended my clinics. They spend tens of thousands of dollars in developing yearly operating plans for their companies, but their blackjack activities are run by the seat of their pants with little or no thought given to why they play or what they intend to get out of it.

Start by writing down your goals and objectives. Be as specific as possible. The best articulation of a goal I have ever heard or read was expressed this way in 1987: "I intend to win $10,000 a year in part-time play until 1990. At that time I plan to move my family to Las Vegas and become a semiprofessional blackjack player earning $50,000 a year or more." This player knew exactly what he wanted— and he accomplished this goal.

Your plan should include a tentative schedule, and it should definitely include your training activities and the level of skill you intend to achieve. It should include all the methods you intend to utilize and it should set forth your bankroll and money-management parameters such as betting units, stop-loss, etc.

Your documented plan does not have to be a pretty typewritten piece. In fact, it is better if it is in your own handwriting. When you write something with your own hand, there is a better connection between this physical act and your brain accepting the idea. It is important that you develop the intention to execute your plan and that this intention is nurtured, survives and becomes real when you take pen or pencil in hand and write down your goals and objectives.

STEP 5: EXECUTE THE PLAN OF ACTION

A plan doesn't mean anything until it's executed. Perhaps it calls for practicing card counting and the Count Reversal System twice a week. The execution is the doing. And you will feel good when you carry out the plan steps.

Execution involves documenting your casino play. You should document every table you play and every session. Your documentation should become a permanent record.

STEP 6: EVALUATE YOUR PROGRESS TOWARD ACCOMPLISHING THE PLAN GOALS AND TAKE CORRECTIVE ACTION AS NECESSARY

This is the most important part of the Planning Process: evaluation, assessment of progress, definition of problems and identification of corrective action. A plan is not a static document put on a shelf and referred to once in a while. A plan changes from feedback to the real world. Steps 4, 5 and 6 are really all part of the planning process: you document your plan; execute it and evaluate it.

This is why it is important to document every table that you play. This is mandatory if this step is to be successfully accomplished.

Examples of Steps 4, 5 and 6 are included as a case study of a successful player in Chapter 18. You will read exactly how these steps are carried out. Do not sluff over this chapter. It may be the most important one in this book.

STEP 7: GIVE A LITTLE BIT BACK BY HELPING AND WORKING WITH OTHER PLAYERS

There is an amazing phenomenon in the game of blackjack. And that is the synergism that occurs when you work with and help a less experienced player. Your own learning and skills are reinforced, and areas of your own play that need practice and attention are exposed. But better yet is the satisfaction you get by helping the less experienced player. I have been encouraging this with my own students for years and it pays off every time. A wise man once said that you never really learn something until you teach it to someone else. Try it! You really can't understand what I am writing about here until you make it real for yourself.

PART FOUR

How to Become a Professional Blackjack Player

17

Considerations on Becoming a Professional Blackjack Player

A FANTASY WORLD AND THE REAL WORLD OF PROFESSIONAL BLACKJACK

There is a fantasy about playing professional blackjack. This is the idea of earning big bucks in a glamorous environment. It's the excitement of taking on the casinos and beating them at their own game. It's the security of having all the money you'll ever need. The fantasy even extends to the jet set. There's the dream of traveling the world, seeing exotic locations, meeting beautiful people and paying all your expenses and then some by playing blackjack.

It's not that easy. Playing blackjack for a living is work the same as holding a job. And there are not that many gamblers who can hold up to the demands of the job.

In the days of the Old West, many pioneers had a dream of finding gold in California or of carving a farm out of the wilderness. They sold everything they had, bought a covered wagon and rolled west with a wagon train. The books that they read never warned them of the hardships along the way. The ones that made it followed a trail littered with broken-down wagons, abandoned furniture, animal carcasses and skeletons of those that fell by the wayside.

I can tell you a hundred stories of the many skeletons along the trail on the road to becoming a professional blackjack player.

There was Steve, for example. He was one of my most successful students in the days when I taught card counting. Single and with no debts or responsibilities, he decided to move to Nevada. Steve was under-bankrolled and he learned the hard way that the 1½% advantage of the card counter does not translate into instant riches. He also found out that the casinos don't like card counters; the pit bosses call them "undesirables" and list them in their black books in the same categories as cheats. Steve was a very disciplined player, but barely earned enough money to support himself. He quickly became fed up with the grind of casino play, returned east and went back to work in the nine-to-five world.

Most of the would-be professionals I know make the move to Nevada. Mark was in this category, and he was under-bankrolled like many of the others. But he had one thing going for him—his wife worked. Mark played for small stakes and did all right in the beginning. But his winnings did not amount to much and he became impatient. Mark decided to take a shot and go for a big win with his small bankroll. Instead he took a hit and got blown out of the water.

Those that fail usually do so because of a lack of knowledge of money management. They get the mistaken idea that a small bankroll can make them rich. And they have no notion of the discipline and mental attitudes that are required to become a successful pro. Their skeletons litter the trail on the way west.

The successful players have two attributes that are mandatory. One is their willingness to hold a part-time or even a full-time job while they build a large enough bankroll to make some big money. The other is their decision to learn how to win in another of the gambling games that Nevada offers.

One player who made it learned how to play poker. He decided that winning money from other gamblers was easier than winning from the blackjack dealers. He continues to win at both the blackjack and poker tables.

Another became a horse handicapper. He spent mornings and some afternoons in the race book making $2 bets as he learned how to handicap. Evenings were spent at the blackjack tables. This person was also under-bankrolled, but he eked out a living for two years before giving up and returning east.

"The Equalizer," who wrote the next chapter, moved to Nevada but held a full-time job for over two years while he built his blackjack bankroll. And he started with a zero bankroll! The Equalizer will teach you two lessons: (1) good discipline and mental preparation can overcome any barrier; and (2) record keeping is mandatory; table-by-table and session summary records are used mainly for self-improvement and corrective action. And corrective action is what it's all about if your goal is to become a consistent, winning player and/or a semiprofessional or professional player.

The most successful "professional" blackjack player I know is a Christmas-tree farmer from the state of Washington. He plays blackjack in the off-season—about half the time. And, when in Nevada, he doesn't play blackjack every day—about three days a week and only six hours on those three days. This person, we'll call him JT, knows his strengths and his weaknesses. He plays to his strengths and respects his weaknesses by following his schedule. This leaves him plenty of time to "smell the roses."

A 4-STAGE PLAN FOR BECOMING A PROFESSIONAL PLAYER

Should you become a professional investor? If you establish this goal, my advice is to proceed in stages. After you have learned the skills discussed in this book, you can establish a *4-Stage Plan* for turning professional.

Before discussing the plan, let me offer a new definition of a professional blackjack player. Playing professionally does not have to mean, in fact should not mean, playing full-time for a living. My definition of a professional is a player who plays serious, plays often and uses blackjack as a means of generating profit to supplement his or her income. In a few cases it will mean playing full-time, but playing full-time only long enough to achieve one or two specific goals. The plan will explain this.

Stage 1

Stage 1 of the plan is to play part-time, acquire enough money to live on for at least six months and build a reasonable-sized bankroll—about $5000. You should also reduce your financial obligations to a minimum. You don't want the pressure of too many monthly payments clouding your judgment.

Stage 1 involves playing part-time for at least a six-month period, perhaps longer. This is a strategy that many East Coast players who live near Atlantic City can easily adopt. Their overhead is low because they can drive down for an evening or weekend session. If you live in a location far from Atlantic City or Nevada, consider other alternatives. Many Indian reservations offer casino blackjack. Casino blackjack is legal in South Dakota and in Iowa. Even though these latter two locations offer a maximum bet of only $5, that's okay because Stage 1 is your test period, to determine whether or not you have the mettle to become a pro. If your blackjack profits are at an acceptable level for this period and you have accumulated the necessary funds, then you can proceed to Stage 2.

At the end of Stage 1, you should have six months of living expenses plus at least a $5000 bankroll. It is recognized that this is difficult to do if you are playing in Deadwood or an Iowa riverboat with a $5 maximum bet. For players in this category, I suggest starting with a small bankroll and doubling it—from $500 to $1000 or from $1000 to $2000. You have to think in terms of units and not dollars. If you are playing with a $5 maximum bet, your betting unit should be $1. With a $500 bankroll, you are playing with 500 betting units and betting from $1 to $5. If you haven't doubled this small bankroll in about 250 hours of play, you probably should forget about turning pro (or get some higher-level instruction).

But if you do double it, look at what you have accomplished. You have won 500 betting units! If your unit was $10 instead of $1, you would have won $5000!

Many would-be professionals will read this page and think to themselves that "Hey, I've got the money now; why wait; I don't need to play blackjack to establish my bankroll." Maybe you don't; but you should. It's as simple as this—if you can't win your bankroll at the tables (with the exception of the $5 maximum bet tables noted above), you probably should not turn pro.

Stage 2

Stage 2 of the plan involves traveling to a remote location for a temporary period of time. Go to Nevada or Atlantic City and play blackjack. Don't quit your job just yet. Take a leave of absence. Wait and see how you do. Now your objective is to make money plus pay for your increased overhead. Return home after the season and evaluate your situation. Is this what you want to do? Are you making enough money? Do you enjoy what you are doing? Do you want to continue in Stage 2 or proceed to Stage 3? Or perhaps even return to Stage 1, where you work part-time and play part-time?

Professional blackjack is work the same as holding a job. Your learning should continue through the two stages described above. You should continue to perfect your techniques and expand and improve your skills. Stay abreast of what's happening in your new career field.

Stage 3

Stage 3 of the plan involves full-time play or serious part-time play and could involve a move to Nevada or Atlantic City. Most professionals choose Nevada over Atlantic City for three reasons: (1) the variety of games offer more opportunities to make money; Atlantic City's games are standard 6- and 8-decks with no rules variations; (2) other opportunities for making money abound; (3) the quality of life is much more pleasant.

Most players who reach Stage 3 have established relationships with at least two other successful players. Many become part of or establish networks of successful players. These connections are not just for team or cooperative play; most players need the emotional support that comes from working with a group of peers.

You don't have to live in Nevada to be a professional, but it helps if you're active in sports betting as I am. There are many beautiful locations in Nevada where you can settle. I chose the Reno area because I like the mountains and the climate. And I have access to the many sports books in the Reno and Lake Tahoe areas, not to mention the best blackjack games in the world.

Stage 4

Stage 4 of the plan is diversification. Choose a game you can beat other than blackjack. Diversification makes life much more interesting. Consider the following alternatives: sports betting, horse handicapping and poker. Each of these games offers much profit potential.

Now, the purpose of this book is not to teach you how to handicap sports or horses, nor is it to teach you how to shoot craps or play poker. But I feel I would be remiss if I did not give you at least a modicum of advice, especially since many of my clients consider me an expert in all of these games except poker. If I can help you avoid the pitfalls and mistakes I made, then these comments will have served their purpose.

Sports betting is my favorite game besides blackjack. But it took me three years to learn how to win. The first mistake I made was assuming that I could quickly learn how to handicap the games and start beating the bookies and the sports books right now. It doesn't work that way, and it cost me thousands of dollars to find that out. The second mistake I made was in believing there were many successful handicappers around and all I had to do was choose one, bet his selections and watch the money roll in. No such luck. There are only a handful of successful handicappers in this country, and few sports touts (handicappers who sell their selections to the betting public) fall into this category. If you are operating in Las Vegas, don't get tangled up with a sports tout! Most of them are pandering to the gambling urge of football, basketball and baseball fans. Their clients don't win, and therefore the touts must advertise frequently to bring in fresh losers—I mean clients—on a continuous basis.

I worked with at least a dozen handicappers before I found one who knows what he is doing and wins on a consistent basis. It took him only ten years to reach this pinnacle! His track record is above 60% in both college and pro football and close to 60% in pro basketball. He is a professional gambler and has plenty of time to devote to sports handicapping. His methods are always evolving, always getting better. He incorporates new methods and techniques into his winning arsenal every year. He truly knows how to stay one step ahead of the linemaker (the person who decides which team is favored to win and by how many points). If you are a sports bettor or would like to become one, please contact me and inquire about my handicapping service. I am not a tout, because I don't advertise for customers. But I don't mind sharing information with my clients. The only games I release are ones I am betting myself. And all clients get the same games.

In summary: If you are going to bet sports, don't try to handicap your own games and don't buy your games from a tout. Find a winning handicapper with a reliable track record and check him out.

I believe that it is easier to handicap the horses than it is to handicap football games. Horses are much more predictable than twenty-two beefy guys running around a football field. You can learn to handicap, but it does take work. There are two main barriers that must be hurdled if you choose this route as your second source of income. The first is the hundreds of systems and methods that abound in this field. Wading through these on your own, finding the methods that really work and separating them from the myriad that are dangled in front of you by the system sellers, with promises of quick riches, could take years. There are only about a half a dozen methods that work on a consistent basis. And there are only two instructors whom you should connect with if you decide to become a horse-race handicapper. I will be happy to put you in touch with either or both of them. Just use the information request form in the back of this book.

The second barrier to becoming a successful horse-race handicapper is discipline. The discipline to analyze large amounts of data and to perform this analysis on a daily basis. There is nothing too complicated about this analysis, but it does take time. Pick up a copy of *The Daily Racing Form* and take a look at just one race therein and you will see what I mean. The numbers make no sense to the inexperienced eye; you must learn to sift out those that are meaningful and subject them to careful scrutiny; you must learn to toss out the losers and narrow a race down to the live contenders.

There is another diversion that bears mentioning at this juncture—casino craps. After many years of research, I and one of my associates have discovered a table-selection and money-management method for winning on a consistent basis. Your inquiries are invited.

The final diversion that many players, myself included, choose are the financial markets. Specifically the stock-options and commodities-futures markets. I am active in these markets on a year-round basis and will be happy to share my methods and information with you. Just use the card in the back of this book to request further information.

You have just finished reading the first chapter of Part IV. Part IV also includes a chapter witten by a part-time professional player and a chapter about my blackjack trip to Macao. Both chapters will assist you in making your decision about your blackjack goals and the extent to which you wish to pursue a professional career.

18

Case Study—A Report to Jerry Patterson on My Goal of Becoming a Professional Blackjack Player by The Equalizer

BACKGROUND

I vividly remember the first blackjack table I ever played. It was late January 1986. I had been playing craps at the Barbary Coast in Las Vegas and had lost all but $3 of my gambling funds. Discouraged, I walked to Little Caesar's while I waited for time to leave for the airport to return home. I sat down beside a $1 blackjack table to rest and one of the players invited me to play with them. I figured I didn't have that much to lose, so I accepted the invitation.

Believe it or not, I didn't even know the object of the game. The other players coached me on each hand. When it was time to leave for the airport, I left the table with $14—a net win of 11 units and I didn't even know how to play!

Well, needless to say, this got my attention fast! Upon returning home, I went to a bookstore and bought Lawrence Revere's book *Playing Blackjack as a Business*. I devoured the book and learned basic strategy and the count. I returned to Las Vegas on March 1st, enthused about the fact that I had finally found a casino game that could be beaten. I played six tables and ended the brief trip with a net win of $35, which was a 10-unit win.

Three more trips to Vegas during March and I was rudely awakened to the fact that *You can lose in blackjack*!?@#! I had lost more than 19 units! However, during my last trip to Vegas in March, another player told me about your book *Blackjack's Winning Formula.* He said that he was using your approach and winning about $1000 each weekend! Well, with that prologue, it didn't take me long to find a copy of your book and inhale it cover to cover!

The discovery that has changed the course of my professional life was made in the back of your book—the four-page description of the new TARGET technique! A phone call and two days later, the treasure arrived and claimed my undivided attention for several days.

On April 5th, I returned to Vegas for my first TARGET session and won . . . and won . . . and won!

One of the principles you explain in your TARGET manual is the importance of documenting one's play. Before my first TARGET session, I had gone back through my five previous trips and recorded the sessions on your forms. From that point forward, with only a few exceptions during the late summer of 1986, I have faithfully recorded each blackjack session that I have played.

Here's a summary of my performance for the entire 1986 period. The first six sessions were dramatically volatile and made virtually no net progress. However, after a few sessions of learning how to apply the TARGET technique, the performance began to produce consistent and predictable results. By the end of 1986 I had completed 51 blackjack sessions, with a net win of 108 units. 67% of my sessions ended in net wins with 29% net losses. The unit size ranged from $1 to $5.

LESSONS FROM FIRST YEAR OF PLAY

At the end of 1986, in the quiet of my home, I reviewed my blackjack records for the first time, with a view to learning from them. The things I learned from my 1986 blackjack play are summarized below:

(1) *Documentation.* The first, and most important, thing I learned was that if you want to learn anything from your play to improve it, you have to keep records. Your principle of documenting your play began to make extremely good sense! Documentation must always be performed in a consistent manner or you will never know your performance. [*Author's Note: This is the "Prime Success Factor" I referred to earlier in the book: Documenting every table and session that you play and using it as a tool to take corrective action.*]

(2) *Consistent Winning.* The second thing that struck home was the realization that I really could consistently play blackjack with an advantage over the casino! The potential of this fact had a dramatic impact on my perception of my economic future. If I could just create a large enough blackjack bank so that my unit size was meaningful, I could actually make a reasonable living playing this game.

(3) *Mental Preparation and Discipline.* The third lesson that 1986 taught me was that this game required more than the technical skills of learning basic strategy, counting techniques and TARGET table selection. All of these techniques can be mastered and played exquisitely and a player can still lose. Why? Because the player must be mentally prepared and disciplined to consistently win!

STARTING WITH A ZERO BANKROLL

I was unable to return to Nevada to continue my blackjack play during the first few months of 1987. Then a job opportunity opened up which would "require" a permanent move to Nevada! It didn't take me long to decide to accept it!

As I prepared to relocate to Nevada, an idea began to formulate in my mind. What if I could "grow" my own blackjack bank from zero to a point where it would be large enough to support a $100 betting unit? I could make a very respectable living. And think of all the lessons I could learn from my documentation as the BJ bank doubled, and doubled, and doubled. . . .

When I finally reached the desired bank size, I would have learned a tremendous amount about how I play and would have fine-tuned my play to a highly predictable level of performance! The lessons would be far more valuable than the $10,000 bank that would result!!

After arriving in Nevada, I visited a number of casinos and asked for their promotional coupons, free nickels, etc. After several stops, I had accumulated $10 of "free casino money." My "experiment" was about to begin!!

On May 6, 1987, I had my first session with the free casino money. Playing with $1 units, I had a 3-unit win. Over the next few sessions, I would add more free casino money from time to time until I had a total of $21 of free casino money in my BJ bank. As it turned out, I did not need any more than the original $10. Later, when I reached a bank size of $100, I withdrew all of the free casino money, which left the BJ bank composed entirely of net winnings! That is the condition of my BJ bank to this day . . . I have absolutely zero dollars of my own invested in my BJ bank!

My performance in 1987 was much more erratic than 1986. The sessions produced a net win of 98 units, with 60% of the sessions ending with a net unit win. Average unit win was 1.85 units per session. The unit size varied from $1 to $3. At the high point, I had reached 131 units net win, then had some radical losses back to 59 units. Just before the end of the year, I had a table which produced a net win of 48 units (my career-high table!) which salvaged the year's overall performance.

LESSONS FROM SECOND YEAR OF PLAY

Again, after the end of 1987, I sat down in the quiet of my home and reviewed that all-important component of my blackjack play— my documentation. I arranged the data in a number of ways, charting it, diagramming it, performing simple statistical analyses of it, and discovered a number of very important items:

(1) *Win Rate Calculation.* I could determine with a reasonable reliability a "win rate" percentage. I estimated my observation how many hands per hour a typical dealer with a half-full table could deal. This number came to about 60 hands per hour to each player. If my average bet size is one unit, then I would typically average 60 units wagered per hour. If I ended the hour with a net win of 2 units, then 2 units divided by 60 units would yield the percentage win rate. In this case, a 3.33% win rate for the hour played. Using this formula, I found that my overall win rate for the entire year was approximately 1.66%. Using this information, I could now project into the future a reasonable expectation of unit and dollar amounts of net win during future periods of time! Predictability at last, and based on my own performance, not someone else's!!

(2) *Maximum Session Time Period.* I analyzed the sessions based on length of session and session performance. I found that for those sessions which lasted more than 90 minutes, my win rate was just under 1%. Those sessions less than 90 minutes had an overall win rate of nearly 6%. My conclusion from this was that performance is higher with shorter sessions. Now my maximum session length is 90 minutes at a time. After that period, I terminate the session and take a meaningful break.

(3) *Maximum Session Stop-Loss.* I analyzed the sessions based on the volatility—that is, how far up and/or down in units the session went and whether I was able to recover from a net loss during the session. I found that in those sessions in which there was a net loss of 10 or more units at any given point, I was able to recover to a winning session finish less than 7% of the time. From this conclusion, I modified my play to limit the amount of units I take with me to 10 units. When those 10 are gone, the session automatically terminates. With further analysis, I have now lowered that to a maximum loss of 6 units in a session and have seen a much more consistent and smoother performance.

(4) *Changing Bet Size with a Growing BJ Bank.* It is very difficult to "grow" a BJ bank from a small beginning because you have to eventually change unit size as the BJ bank grows. When you go from a $1 unit to a $2 unit, it is a 100% increase, whereas changing from

$10 to $11 is only a 10% increase. You usually increase unit size right after a series of winning sessions, which brings you to the next increment for changing unit size.

However, statistically, after several winning sessions, you are due for a losing session. The losing session, occurring right after you increase unit size, causes a dramatic loss in dollars in the bank even though the unit loss is not inordinately high! This means that extreme caution must be used when increasing unit size based on a higher BJ bank balance. I have still, after much experimentation, not developed a formula which is entirely satisfactory in knowing how to move unit size up or down.

LESSONS FROM THIRD YEAR OF PLAY

1987 had resulted in a net unit win of 98 units. My BJ bank size was now at $100.75 after about seven months of the "experiment," all of it net winnings! After careful analysis of 1987 performance, I set a goal of 200 units. This, I estimated, would result in a BJ bank at the end of 1988 of about $500, with the increase of unit size as the bank grew.

Modifications I implemented during this year of play resulted in a smoother, more consistent progression in units. There were no major slumps, although one or two periods produced rather level activity without any net gains.

By the end of the year, I had achieved a net win of 228 units, surpassing my goal of 200 units. The BJ bank had grown to $743.75 on December 31st. In both units and dollars, I had exceeded expectations. The performance was smoother and more predictable. It was now coming together at last!

In January 1988, I had projected that it would take me 115 sessions and playing time of 172.5 hours to reach the 200 units. It turned out that it took me 139 sessions and 99.6 hours of playing time. One reason for this discrepancy was that my average session length had shortened to about 45 minutes.

Now . . . this is becoming a habit! Most people have New Year's resolutions. I have a New Year's Blackjack Analysis! Although it is impossible to list all of the lessons the year brought, below are some of them, derived, again, from my documentation:

(1) *Lower Volatility.* By reducing my session playing bank from 10 units to 6 units during the year, I was able to reduce the wide swings in the units won/lost and bank balance. This helped fine-tune my play.

(2) *Increased Confidence.* The greatest confidence builder was comparing my historical performance with that of Lawrence Revere, author of *Playing Blackjack as a Business.* I was able to chart his performance from Page 141 of his book in a reasonably comparable manner to my own charts and "overlay" his performance for the 190 days with a similar period of my own. The result was that, if you took the names off the charts, you could not tell which chart was mine and which was Revere's! I must be doing something right!!

(3) *Predictability.* After three years of history, I can now say that I consistently play at a win rate of 2.5% to 3.0% and I can, by using my documentation as a foundation, project an hourly win rate in units and dollars and "budget," if you will, the time required to produce a required amount of winnings!

(4) *Emotional Discipline.* Most importantly, 1988 saw me reach the point where the emotional swings caused by winning or losing have leveled out and have been replaced with a disciplined and rational approach to the game. The mental game came together. I can determine, by means of my documentation, when it is statistically appropriate for a losing session or winning session to occur. When losing sessions do occur, it does not cause either doubt or depression because I can see from my documentation that the identical swings in wins and losses have occurred in the past and will occur again in the future. I just keep pressing on and make sure the play is technically accurate!

By the end of 1988, I had established for myself that I had the technical and emotional capacity to play professional-level blackjack. Now it is just a matter of time until the BJ bank reached the level which will justify the optimum unit size of $100.

I have also augmented my documentation so I can track my performance in each casino that I play. I now can observe that in some casinos, I am playing at a better than 10% win rate and at others a consistently negative rate of 5% or more. I am not sure how I will modify my play based on this information yet, but I'm sure that my documentation will give me guidance on this issue as well!

By the way, the pen name I have adopted, The Equalizer, has come from this new documentation of individual casino perform-ance. You see, as I observe my records, I find that I am simply taking money from one casino, depositing it with another casino, and taking a 3% "vigorish" (commission) for the effort. Thus, without my "assistance," some casinos would have more money than others. I am simply EQUALIZING the funds of the various casinos!!

Early in 1989 I implemented rigid enforcement of a new princi-ple: locking in a minimum of one-unit win when a 2-unit win has been achieved at a table and not bringing the locked-up units out for any purpose.

During the first 13 sessions of using this principle, my unit win rate jumped to over 4 units per hour with a win rate of 6.24%. My table win rate is over 61% rather than the typical 42% and my session win rate is 77% rather than the typical 62%.

This is a major result of my new principle: Locking in the one-unit win cuts off the bottom part of the natural curve of winning/losing that occurs at a table, even a TARGET table. The results are a dramatic increase in the win rate but a substantial reduction in hands played at each table.

I have noticed that I am spending a greater percentage of my time scouting, not because I cannot find tables, but because I leave the tables I find much more quickly, with a small win in most cases. For example, during the last two sessions, the session length was 51 minutes combined total. However, I played only two tables with a total of 11 hands played. Yet I achieved a net win of 3.6 units. That means that my win rate for the actual playing time was 32.7%. The hourly win rate for the sessions was 4.2 units per hour. The same kind of results seem to be evidenced in the other sessions since starting this principle.

After 20 sessions using this principle, my results are as follows:

- Session Win Rate: 75%
- Table Win Rate: 52%

- Hourly Win Rate: 4.8%
- Units Won Per Hour: 2.9%

I intend to continue these results into the 1990s and to accomplish my goal of becoming a professional blackjack player!

19

Blackjack Trip to Macao From Jerry Patterson's Blackjack Diary

JERRY PATTERSON'S TRAVEL SCENARIO

Macao. A small, Portuguese-controlled city on the southern tip of the Canton peninsula in China. About forty miles and fifty-five minutes by jetfoil from Hong Kong. Blackjack is played in Macao. And it is unlike any game in the world. You've got to see this game to believe it. Beatable? Maybe. But before I go into detail, let me give you some background.

As a professional blackjack player for over ten years, I am very fortunate. Because I live less than fifty miles from Atlantic City, my overhead is nil—gas money and that's it. My other advantage is time. I can leave my home at 7 P.M. and be sitting at a blackjack table by 8:15. So I don't have to spend large amounts of time, as some players do, getting to and from my place of work.

Kenny Uston, God rest his soul, did me a favor when he took on the Atlantic City casinos and the New Jersey State Supreme Court. They upheld his right to play without getting barred. So I play with impunity. Some of the casinos know who I am and some don't. I can beat some of the casinos and some I can't. I stick with the ones I can beat. After all, there are over 800 blackjack tables to choose from!

But now back to Macao. When I take an exotic trip like this, I have other objectives than winning money: a vacation, new experiences, a reward for doing well at home, the fulfillment of a desire to explore different cultures and cuisines, the making of new friends. Quite honestly, it's difficult to make any big money playing blackjack in foreign locations, at least for me. The problem is the expenses in getting there. When I travel abroad, my objective is to make expenses—and maybe pay for a shopping spree or two.

And when I travel, I travel first class. I stay at the best hotels. I eat at the finest restaurants. Unlike two other well-known blackjack authors, I am not a "coupon player." I don't account for every penny and I don't mind spending money. As a matter of fact, my win in Macao did not even cover my expenses for this fantastic trip. But so what? I can always pick them up in Atlantic City when I get back.

Nancy and I decided on the spur of the moment to visit Hong Kong and Macao. As our decision was made around Christmastime, it was very difficult to secure accommodations. With a Christian population of only 10%, it is surprising how popular Hong Kong is during the Christmas holidays.

From Philadelphia International, we connected with a Canadian Pacific flight out of Toronto and landed in Hong Kong some twenty hours and one lost day later. (You lose a day going but gain it coming back.)

A WORLD-CLASS HOTEL

After clearing customs, we were delighted to find The Peninsula hotel's limousine waiting to pick us up. Twenty minutes later, we checked in to one of the top ten hotels of the world. The British Colonial motif is still very much in evidence at "The Pen." High ceilings and tall pillars dominate the spacious lobby. Tables and chairs abound and many guests were having tea even at our 8:00 P.M. check-in time.

But service is what a world-class hotel is all about, and our high expectations were not disappointed. Little things like a basket of fruit and a bottle of champagne were provided upon our arrival. We were shown to our room by a uniformed reception clerk. Our beds were turned down every evening and a paper waited for us every morning. And we rarely had to even open the door to our room. Joe, our morning boy, or Stan, our evening boy, was usually right there to open the door for us. And they took care of our every need, from getting shoes shined to mending a torn shirt.

After a Christmas Eve stroll to enjoy the beautiful Christmas lights and decorations of the Kowloon shopping district (even more beautiful than the lights of New York City, by the way), we even found a small stocking laying on our pillows, stuffed with fruits and Christmas candies.

One of the most enjoyable parts of our stay at The Peninsula was the Christmas Day party hosted by the hotel manager. Champagne, cocktails and delicious hors d'oeuvres were served as we chatted with the other international guests.

However, this is not a chapter about The Pen. It is about blackjack in Macao. But please permit a tourist his diversions before we get to the blackjack stories.

TWO TOURISTS IN HONG KONG

One of our objectives on this trip was to experience all of the sensuous delights of Hong Kong. Now, I'm not much for guided tours with other American tourists, although there is a time and place when these tours are appropriate. Hong Kong is not one of them. With probably the most efficient rapid transit system in the world, it is very easy to establish one's itinerary in the morning and then, traveling by train, tram (streetcar) or bus, experience the various sights throughout the day.

We took a tram ride from one end of Hong Kong Island to the other. Starting in the Western District, we wound our way through the myriad small shops, narrow streets and alleys and the hodge-podge of neon signs. The shops offered everything from expensive antiques to used tires to live chickens, whose necks would be wrung at your request prior to taking one home for dinner.

I'm not going to give you a detailed account of our tourist activities, but there are a few more highlights I would like to mention before we depart on the jetfoil for Macao.

When in Hong Kong, there are certain things that you absolutely must do. One of them is to take a trip to the Aberdeen District—a fascinating harbor area with seemingly hundreds of sampans (small boats lived on by Chinese fishermen) and a delightful floating restaurant. Take a tour of the harbor on a sampan and observe the boat people. If you are in the harbor area, you will be accosted by many of them offering to take you on a tour in their sampan. A half-hour tour will cost less than $10. You can bargain with them, but at this price, why not give them what they ask? They need the money more than you do.

Another thing you must do is to experience the cuisine. Most people like Chinese food and I am no exception. But, unlike Nancy, I don't like to eat it every day. So we agreed while enroute and planning our itinerary that we would sample at least one of the other many fine gourmet restaurants in Hong Kong.

It turned out to be The Pierrot—a restaurant high atop The Mandarin Hotel—rated one of the top ten hotels in the world and the one in which we stayed upon our return from Macao. In my book, The Pierrot matches the hotel's status in a list of the world's top ten restaurants. Although staffed by Chinese waiters, the Pierrot is very French and made a very good first impression upon us when we were greeted by a French maître d' with a delightful accent.

I started with a crab soup flavored with fresh tarragon and mango. It was delicious and unlike anything I'd ever had before. The soup was not thick, which seemed to magnify the taste sensations I experienced.

My main course was roast turbot with red onions and a Burgundy wine sauce. Soft and flaky, the mild and pleasant fishy taste was well complemented by the generous portions of red onions. For dessert, I ordered a "floating island"; poached egg whites in a vanilla sauce with pistachios. The dessert was perfect for lunch—very light, very tasty, but not too sweet. We topped off the lunch with a delicious café au lait.

ON TO MACAO

I departed for Macao on Christmas Day on the 6 P.M. jetfoil with a return ticket for thirty-nine hours later on Sunday morning at 9

A.M. Mentally, I prepared myself for the masses of people who would be crowding the blackjack tables.

The following were some thoughts crossing my mind en route to Macao. In the late 1970s, Macao had the best blackjack game in the world. They had rules that were unimaginable in this country. Early surrender anytime (the dealer did not take a hole card), not just on your first two cards, but even after a split or double down. Double down on any number of cards. All kinds of neat bonus rules for special hands such as 6, 7, 8. A half-win surrender on 5-card hands. And a number of other very positive rules that I can't even remember.

Stanford Wong wrote a book called *Blackjack in Asia.* He wrote about this game and other "candy stores" in Korea, the Philippines and Indonesia. Wong sold the book for $2000 a copy. He told me at the time that he sold a total of five books, including one to an American blackjack team that eventually burned out the favorable game in Macao by winning over one million Hong Kong dollars (about $150,000).

I have always wondered why Wong did this. Why would a guy sell out a game for $10,000 that could have produced hundreds of thousands of dollars of winnings per year? The only reason I can figure is that he took a $10,000 or so hit—as documented in this book—and got fed up and decided not to go back.

After arrival I hired a bicycle-ridden rickshaw to transport me to the Oriental Macau Hotel—nothing like The Pen but very comfortable and perfectly suitable for my thirty-six-hour stay.

After a quick dinner at the hotel, I took a cab down to the Lisboa Hotel and Casino. From the outside, this place is a monstrosity. It's an ugly building, circular in shape, needing a paint job, and with a monstrous roulette wheel perched on top!

I played blackjack this first evening and all the next day. But before I describe the game, let me share with you just a few impressions of this interesting city.

The best way to see Macao is simply to stroll around. I enjoyed strolling along the waterfront and observing the ancient colonial homes and buildings, some waterside and some perched high on a cliff overlooking the bay. The pace here is totally different from Hong Kong—none of the hustle and bustle in the cobbled streets— no one in a hurry to get anywhere. I found it fascinating to peer through open doorways into the sweatshops where some of the world's cheapest clothing is manufactured.

BLACKJACK IN MACAO

It will take a few paragraphs to describe what I found. Let's divide this description into three parts: (1) Blackjack Rules, (2) The Play of the Hand, and (3) The Shuffle.

Blackjack Rules

- Double Down on 11 only.
- Resplitting pairs okay but with only one card on each split ace.
- Doubling down after splitting permitted on the 11.
- Early surrender against all up cards except an ace.
- 5-card half-win surrender except against an ace.
- Dealer stands on soft 17.
- Dealer takes no hole card until after players play their hands (except on an ace).
- Dealer checks for blackjack with ace showing after players exercise insurance option and before players play their hands.
- Player sitting at table may play only one hand.
- Any player, at table or behind, may bet on as many other players' hands as he or she desires.
- The high bet controls the play of the hand.
- Insurance permitted.
- Cards dealt face-down from a six-deck covered shoe (you can't see the cards in this shoe).
- No visible discard tray; it is built under the table so that the discards are also hidden from view.
- About a half-deck cut off from the back of the shoe and one card

burned before each round and before the dealer takes her hole card.

Other than the double-down rule and the hidden cards, these rules are not all that unfavorable and present some interesting possibilities for a winning strategy that we will discuss later.

The Play of the Hand

Dealer deals two face-down cards to each player. Dealer folds her (all the dealers are female) hands and rests while players squeeze cards. The Chinese love to squeeze their cards, and you now have to exercise patience while this tradition unfolds for each hand. They pick up their two cards so that only the front card is visible. Then they squeeze the two cards so that the unseen card comes slowly into view. When they finally see the second card, they gently lay the two cards down, face-up, in front of their bet in the betting circle.

After I accepted the fact that only about twenty hands an hour would be dealt, I got into the spirit of this interesting tradition and enjoyed the process of squeezing my own two cards. It is especially fun when the top card is a 10 or an ace, because then you are trying to squeeze out a blackjack!

After all the players have laid down their two cards, the dealer proceeds to first base. Before the dealer deals to first base (the player to the dealer's immediate left, who plays his hand first), you must exercise your surrender option if you plan to do so. You cannot surrender your hand when it is your turn to play.

Here is the procedure for taking a hit. You pick up one of your two cards and gently tap the table with it. The dealer will deal you a down card. Then you place your face-up card under this new card so that the faces of these two cards are resting against each other. Then you turn the two cards over and squeeze again so that the new card will slowly come into view. When you see your new card and want another hit, you lay one of your two cards down, face-up, by your other face-up card, and repeat the process with the one card you are still holding.

I saw some players take almost a full minute to play their hands, especially when they were considering a 5-card half-win surrender. And, like the other players, I found myself leaning to my right or left to examine the other player's card as the squeezing process brought it into view. It is as if each new card were a momentous event and therefore must be pondered and carefully studied in its own unit of time.

If you go for the half-win surrender with your 5-cards totaling less than 21, you declare your intentions immediately. The dealer will pay you half your bet, pick up your cards and move on to the next player.

Now, after you have finished playing your hand, the dealer will rearrange your cards into the appropriate pattern before moving on to the next player. All 3-card hands are arranged with two cards together above your bet with the third card tucked underneath, exactly in the middle. Each 4- and 5-card hand has similar patterns. When I first witnessed this interesting practice, I thought that the dealers were adding up the value of the hands while putting them into their patterns. Then I realized that this was not the reason. All of the dealers were Oriental, mostly Chinese, and they were more interested in the symmetry and orderliness of the patterns.

Here is how you play off another player's hand. You reach over his or her shoulder and place your bet inside the winning figure; it wasn't a circle or square—I believe it was a heart. If there is no room inside the figure, just lay your bet down close to the other bets. You may do this at any time before the round is dealt; it is not necessary to ask. If your bet is the high bet, the player sitting in the chair will defer to you when it is his or her turn to play the hand. I never saw any problem with the control of the hand or with the payoffs. The dealer pays each bet separately and, if there is a crowd of players playing off a hot hand, many times the player seated will give back the winning bets to the players standing. I am still amazed that I did not see one argument from a standing playing not getting a proper payoff.

I did not see many European faces in the Lisboa or in the other three casinos in Macao. Macao is a playground for the six million Chinese who live in Hong Kong, so 99% of the players were Chinese. And most speak little or no English, so I did not have the opportunity to talk with many of them. But they were still very, very friendly and accepted me with smiles into their game with no hesitation. And, of course, there is a universal language among blackjack players, especially when the table gets hot and the dealer breaks hand after hand. In happy situations like these, words are unnecessary to communicate.

When you are dealt a blackjack or are on a winning streak with your chips piling up, the dealer is not hesitant about asking for a tip. When dealing to many of the Chinese players, the extra half-win on the blackjack is regarded by the dealer as her money and she doesn't hesitate to take it without even a thank you. The players say nothing and accept this practice as normal procedure. On my biggest win, I was betting stacks of HK$100 chips. On the payoff, the dealer would break one down to smaller chips and blandly ask for a tip. I must say that I did not conform to this "Oriental custom." I did tip the dealer when I left the table with my big win.

The Shuffle

When the all-white cut card is dealt from the shoe, the round is finished and the shuffle procedure commences. Because of the extended duration of the shuffle, about eight to ten minutes, most players leave a small coin near their betting figure and take a break. The dealer relaxes for a few moments by sipping from a cup of tea. She may chat with the second dealer at the table or the male pit person while sipping her tea. All tables have two dealers—one dealing and one sitting and handling the placement of money into the drop box and operating the shuffle machine, which we will get to in just a few moments.

Can you imagine an Atlantic City casino or a Nevada casino putting up with all this down time? The dealer would be fired in minutes!

Eventually the dealer gets around to removing the cards from the shoe and spreads them on the table in three rows for a very extensive "wash." Then, dividing the stacked six decks into two 3-deck piles, she picks about a half-deck in each hand and shuffles these two stacks together six or eight times. In a very relaxed way, very slowly, very methodically, with gaps of only one or two cards as the cards are shuffled together. You don't hear any sound during this procedure—as you would normally hear the "tatatatatata" of the cards being shuffled in an American casino. The cards simply fall from the dealer's hand onto the table. I was fascinated as I watched the lengthy process.

This entire procedure is repeated after the six decks have been shuffled one time through. Then the second dealer get involved and does her thing. She stuffs the cards in picks of about a deck through a small electrical card shuffler.

The cards arc then placed back in the shoe and four to eight cards are burned before play begins again.

This is the most extensive shuffle I have ever seen in any casino. It fosters good distribution of the 10s and aces and very little like-card clumping.

HOW TO WIN IN MACAO

The majority of my win came from looking for and playing off the hot hands. I looked for tables with biases resulting from the non-random shuffle. In many cases, biases favoring the players will transcend the shuffle and come right back in the next shoe. But not so in Macao. Each shoe has to be treated as a separate cycle. And each player's hand can be treated as a separate subcycle. Find a player who's winning and the chances are that he will continue to win.

If you're a card counter, this is one of the few games anywhere that can be beaten by traditional card-counting techniques. Stand behind a table where play is commencing from a fresh shoe, count the cards and keep a running count. Use the High-Low System: 2-6 = + 1; 7, 8, 9 = 0; tens and aces = −1.

When your running count totals 6 or more, play off the hand that appears to be winning the most money. If your bankroll permits, try to make the highest bet so you can control the play of the hand. Continue to keep the running count. Play off one or more hands, all seven if you have the bankroll, as long as the running count stays above 6 and your stop-loss is not exceeded. If the running count falls below 6, or you have lost between 3 and 6 betting units (if you are playing more than one hand, your stop-loss is twice the number of hands played in betting units), discontinue play for this shoe and find a table where the shuffle has just been completed.

TIPS ON PLAYING BLACKJACK IN FOREIGN LOCATIONS

Find out the rules, if at all possible, beforehand. In this way you will know what kind of game you are playing against.

Carefully formulate your objectives for the trip. Vacation? Learning experience? Or to make money with long hours at the tables? There is only one foreign location that is worth the time and overhead for a pure blackjack trip—Seoul, Korea. The rules there are excellent and you can bet any amount you want with impunity.

Establish your blackjack schedule before arrival. Allow at least a day for your body to eliminate the jet lag. Get plenty of sleep that first day.

Learn the local money customs. Understand the conversion rate between dollars and the local currency. When you translate your betting unit into the foreign currency, you must understand exactly how much you are betting. Play with a small unit until you are comfortable with the local currency.

Find out if there will be potential problems in converting local currency back to dollars and transporting the dollars out of the country. Some countries have foreign currency restrictions and you may have trouble getting a big win out of the country.

Convert your trip money into American Express Traveler's Checks before departure.

PART FIVE

For Beginners and Less-Experienced Players

20

How to Play This Game

RULES OF PLAY

The game of blackjack is played with one to eight decks of cards. After shuffling, the cards are hand-dealt (one or two decks) or dealt from a box called a shoe. Usually, from half to three-quarters of the cards are dealt before shuffling and starting a new game.

Before a new game begins, the dealer spreads the cards to be used across the table, first face-down so the backs can be inspected for telltale markings, and then face-up, enabling both the dealer and the players to ascertain that there are no extra or missing cards. Standard 52-card poker-sized decks are used, and the four suits have no significance; only the numerical value of each card is important: 2s through 9s are counted at their point value, and all 10s and face cards are valued at 10. The ace is unique, and can be counted as one or 11 at the player's option.

Blackjack

After receiving your initial two cards from the dealer, you determine their value by simply adding them together. A 5 and 3 is 8, a king and 6 is 16, and an ace and 7 is either 8 or 18. If your first two cards consist of an ace and a 10 or any picture card, the hand is a perfect one—a "blackjack"—often called a natural. Unless the dealer ties you with another blackjack, you have an automatic winner, and instead of the usual even-money payoff, you are immediately paid one and a half times your bet—if you have $10 up, you receive $15. With a tie, called a *push*, no money is exchanged.

Hard and Soft Hands

All hands not containing an ace are known as *hard* hands, and any hand including an ace that can be valued as 11 is called a *soft* hand. For example, an A-5 is a soft 16; if hit with a 2, the hand becomes a soft 18; if another card is drawn, for instance a 9, the ace is revalued as one (if it were valued as 11 you would "break") and the final hand now becomes a hard 17. Any hard hand of 12 through 16 is known as a "stiff," or breaking hand, because it is possible to go over 21 with the addition of one more card.

Objective

Let's now consider the objective of casino blackjack. Many blackjack books define the objective as getting a hand as close as possible to 21. This is not always true. **Your objective is to beat the dealer,** and learning this lesson is your first step on the road to becoming a winning blackjack player. It is possible to beat the dealer by holding a hand that totals less than 21—a 12 or 13, for example. Remember there are two ways to win: by holding a hand higher than the dealer, and by not hitting a breaking hand and waiting for the dealer to break. This is a decision that many beginning players seldom make. Thinking they must always get as close as possible to 21, they hit (take extra cards) more often than they should, thus breaking (a hand with a value greater than 21), losing more often and contributing to the casino edge of up to 6% over the nonsystem player.

Casino rules are defined to give the dealer one major advantage and one major disadvantage. The advantage is that the dealer always draws last. If he breaks after you have broken—in reality a tie—he has already collected your chips, and he does not return them. The dealer's disadvantage is that he *must draw* if he has 16 or less; therefore, with hands totaling 12 to 16, it's possible that the next card may break him. You, the player, can capitalize on this handicap by making judicious decisions about drawing or standing.

While many players lose because they hit too often, other novices, unrealistically hoping for the dealer to break, do not hit enough. These hitting and standing decisions cannot be made by hunch; logic must be used. If the dealer's up-card is 2, 3, 4 or 5, you know he must hit, no matter what the value of his hole (face-down) card is; therefore, you should *stand* (refuse any additional cards) on a lower hand value, such as 13, and hope for the dealer to break. On the other hand, if the dealer has a high up-card, for instance a 9 or 10, you would hit to try to get as close to 21 as possible, because there is a good chance the dealer's hole card is also high, and with a hand greater than 16, the dealer must stand. After making your hit-and-stand decisions, if you haven't broken, you wait for the dealer to deal to the other players and then to himself. Then your bet is paid off at even money if you win, collected if you lose, or left alone if you tie.

Options

The characteristic that makes blackjack unique among all casino games is the many player options. After you receive your first two cards, in addition to the option of hitting and standing, under certain conditions you are allowed to split your hand, double your bet, insure your hand, or, if you are not satisfied with your cards, sometimes you can surrender them and get half your money back. Almost all decisions are indicated to the dealer by the way you move your hand or where you place additional chips after your original wager is made. Let's look at these decisions and their signals; just remember in Atlantic City and many other places where multi-decks are used, you are never permitted to touch your cards or your initial bet.

Standing

The player always has the option of standing at any time. In Atlantic City casinos as well as in many others, you must give a hand signal rather than a verbal signal. To indicate to the dealer that you wish to stand, simply wave your hand, palm down, over your cards. The dealer will then move on to the next player. In many Nevada games the cards are dealt face-down and the players pick them up to play the hand. A standing signal in this game is given by tucking the first two cards dealt (the ones you are holding in your hand) under your chips.

Hitting

If you are not satisfied with the total of your hand, you may draw one or more cards, as long as you don't break or go over 21. To call for a hit in a face-up game, either point at your cards or make a beckoning motion with your fingers. In the Nevada face-down game, scrape your two cards toward you on the felt to call for a hit. When the hit card breaks your hand, turn your cards over and drop them on the table; the dealer will automatically scoop up your bet and place your cards in the discard tray, as you have lost, even if the dealer subsequently breaks.

Splitting Pairs

When the first two cards you receive are of equal value, you may elect to split them and play each as a separate hand, drawing until you are satisfied or break. You play first the card on your right, and then the card on your left. Two 10-value cards, such as a king and a jack, can also be split, but when aces are split, most casinos permit only one card to be drawn to each. If a 10-value card is drawn to a split ace, or vice versa, the resulting hand is considered a 21, not a blackjack, and is paid off at 1 to 1. This 21 would tie any dealer 21 but would lose to a dealer blackjack. In many casinos, if a pair is split and a third card of the same rank is drawn, the hand may be resplit. However, this is not permitted in Atlantic City. To indicate to the dealer your desire to split, merely slide up another bet of equal value next to your first wager, touching neither your cards nor the original bet. In the Nevada face-down game, just turn over your pair and put out the extra bet. In some casinos, including those in Atlantic City, you may double down after you split. This procedure is explained next. (See page 220)

Doubling Down

After receiving your first two cards, and when you believe you will beat the dealer with just one more card, you are allowed to double your original bet and draw one and only one more card. While many casinos will permit you to double down on any initial hand except two cards totaling 21, some restrict this option to hands that total 10 or 11. To signal the dealer your intention to double, place another bet, up to the amount of the original wager, alongside your first bet. In the Nevada face-down game, turn your two cards over and put out your extra bet. Since you will always have the advantage when you take this option, you should double for the full amount. Again, to minimize the chances for player cheating, you are not permitted to touch either your cards or your original bet. When you split a pair, many casinos will permit you to double down after you draw the first card to each of the split hands.

Insurance

Whenever the dealer's up-card is an ace, before proceeding with the hand, he or she will ask, "Insurance, anyone?" If you believe the

Splits   Double Down

dealer's hole card is a 10 for blackjack, you are permitted to place a side bet up to half of your original wager on the Insurance line in front of you. If, indeed, the dealer does have a 10 in the hole, you are immediately paid 2 to 1 on your insurance bet, but lose your original wager unless you too have blackjack and tie the dealer. You are not really insuring anything; you are simply betting that the dealer's unseen card is a 10. The only time I recommend taking insurance is when you have a blackjack and are past the third level of a winning progression (a succession of winning hands). I'll discuss winning progressions later in this chapter.

Surrender

A few casinos offer the option of surrender. If you are not satisfied with your chances of beating the dealer after seeing your first two cards, you may announce "Surrender"; the dealer will pick up your cards and collect half your bet, returning the other half to you. This is your only decision in blackjack that is indicated verbally. Where the dealer is required to first check his hole card for blackjack, the option is called "late surrender." If you are permitted to turn in your hand before the dealer checks for blackjack, the decision is termed "early surrender." In many casinos, you must announce your surrender decision before the dealer deals to the first hand.

Dealer's Play

After offering cards to all players, the dealer exposes his hole card. If there are players who still have not broken, the dealer then acts on his hand according to fixed rules, with none of the player options. When the dealer's cards total 17 or more, he must stand, and with a hand of 16 or less, the dealer must hit until he reaches 17 or better.

If the dealer breaks, all remaining players win. In most casinos, the dealer must count an ace in his hand as 11 if it will raise his hand to 17, 18, 19, 20 or 21. A few casinos make an exception to this rule and require the dealer to hit A-6, or soft 17. It is important to note that the dealer has no choice in the matter. If all the players have hands totaling 18, 19, 20 or 21, the dealer must still stand with a 17—an obvious loser. Likewise, if the players show hands totaling 12, 13, 14 or 15, the dealer must still hit his 16 and risk breaking an otherwise winning hand.

If the dealer does not break, and reaches a hand between 17 and 21, proceeding counterclockwise from third base (the player to the dealer's immediate right who played his hand last), he collects from players with lower hands, pays off at even money the players with higher hands, and pushes or ties those with equal hands, indicating this with a tap of the back of his fingers in front of the player's cards. Players are now free to pick up winnings, if any, and make a new bet as the whole process is repeated.

THE BASIC STRATEGY FOR PLAYING THE HANDS

Most occasional gamblers are unaware of the tremendous amount of research that has been done to provide blackjack players with winning strategies. This research has been performed with the aid of high-speed computers by some of the best mathematical minds in the country.

The resulting strategy, designed to win more of your good hands and lose fewer of your bad hands, yields the best, or most profitable, decisions applying to all the blackjack options—standing, hitting, splitting, doubling and surrendering. To understand the strategy, though, you must remember the three variables involved in making blackjack decisions—your two cards and the dealer's up-card. There are 550 possible combinations of these three variables; therefore, there are 550 different blackjack decisions. Fortunately, many of these decisions are similar, and about thirty rules cover all of them.

Basic strategy tables on the following pages cover multi-deck (shoe) games for both Atlantic City and Las Vegas and single-deck games for Las Vegas rules and northern Nevada rules. Learn the basic strategy that applies to the casino location that you will be visiting most often.

The small differences between the strategies result from the use of more decks in the game and the rules variations between the locations. In general the multi-deck strategy is more conservative than the single-deck strategy. An example is the player hand of 11 vs. a dealer up-card of ace. In the single-deck game, with just 52 cards, the player has a better chance of drawing the 10, so the correct basic-strategy play is to double down. More cards in the shoe game reduces the player's chances of drawing the 10, so the correct play is to hit.

The main difference between the Atlantic City and Las Vegas Shoe Strategies is a rule variation: in Atlantic City the player is allowed to double down after splitting pairs; in Las Vegas this is allowed in only a few casinos. What this rule variation means is that in Atlantic City the player will split more pairs because of the advantage of doubling after splitting. A pair of 4s, for example, would be split in Atlantic City but hit in Las Vegas.

Many blackjack books advise you to never deviate from basic strategy. Their reasoning is that you should always make the correct mathematical play for each and every hand. This reasoning is correct if you play for the long run. In this book, however, I am teaching

CHART 7

BASIC STRATEGY FOR THE MULTI-DECK SHOE GAME (DOUBLING DOWN AFTER SPLITTING PERMITTED)

THE DEALER'S UP-CARD

YOUR HAND	2	3	4	5	6	7	8	9	10	A
8	H	H	H	H	H	H	H	H	H	H
9	H	D	D	D	D	H	H	H	H	H
10	D	D	D	D	D	D	D	D	H	H
11	D	D	D	D	D	D	D	D	D	H
12	H	H	S	S	S	H	H	H	H	H
13	S	S	S	S	S	H	H	H	H	H
14	S	S	S	S	S	H	H	H	H	H
15	S	S	S	S	S	H	H	H	H	H
16	S	S	S	S	S	H	H	H	H	H
17	S	S	S	S	S	S	S	S	S	S
A,2	H	H	H	D	D	H	H	H	H	H
A,3	H	H	H	D	D	H	H	H	H	H
A,4	H	H	D	D	D	H	H	H	H	H
A,5	H	H	D	D	D	H	H	H	H	H
A,6	H	D	D	D	D	H	H	H	H	H
A,7	S	D	D	D	D	S	S	H	H	H
A,8	S	S	S	S	S	S	S	S	S	S
A,9	S	S	S	S	S	S	S	S	S	S
A,A	P	P	P	P	P	P	P	P	P	P
2,2	P	P	P	P	P	P	H	H	H	H
3,3	P	P	P	P	P	P	H	H	H	H
4,4	H	H	H	P	P	H	H	H	H	H
6,6	P	P	P	P	P	H	H	H	H	H
7,7	P	P	P	P	P	P	H	H	H	H
8,8	P	P	P	P	P	P	P	P	P	P
9,9	P	P	P	P	P	S	P	P	S	S
10,10	S	S	S	S	S	S	S	S	S	S

H = Hit. S = Stand. D = Double Down. P = Split.

CHART 8

BASIC STRATEGY FOR THE MULTI-DECK SHOE GAME (NO DOUBLE DOWN AFTER SPLIT)

THE DEALER'S UP-CARD

YOUR HAND	2	3	4	5	6	7	8	9	10	A
8	H	H	H	H	H	H	H	H	H	H
9	H	D	D	D	D	H	H	H	H	H
10	D	D	D	D	D	D	D	D	H	H
11	D	D	D	D	D	D	D	D	D	H
12	H	H	S	S	S	H	H	H	H	H
13	S	S	S	S	S	H	H	H	H	H
14	S	S	S	S	S	H	H	H	H	H
15	S	S	S	S	S	H	H	H	H	H
16	S	S	S	S	S	H	H	H	H	H
17	S	S	S	S	S	S	S	S	S	S
A,2	H	H	H	D	D	H	H	H	H	H
A,3	H	H	H	D	D	H	H	H	H	H
A,4	H	H	D	D	D	H	H	H	H	H
A,5	H	H	D	D	D	H	H	H	H	H
A,6	H	D	D	D	D	H	H	H	H	H
A,7	S	D	D	D	D	S	S	H	H	H
A,8	S	S	S	S	S	S	S	S	S	S
A,9	S	S	S	S	S	S	S	S	S	S
A,A	P	P	P	P	P	P	P	P	P	P
2,2	H	H	P	P	P	P	H	H	H	H
3,3	H	H	P	P	P	P	H	H	H	H
4,4	H	H	H	H	H	H	H	H	H	H
6,6	H	P	P	P	P	H	H	H	H	H
7,7	P	P	P	P	P	P	H	H	H	H
8,8	P	P	P	P	P	P	P	P	P	P
9,9	P	P	P	P	P	S	P	P	S	S
10,10	S	S	S	S	S	S	S	S	S	S

H = Hit. S = Stand. D = Double Down. P = Split.

CHART 9

BASIC STRATEGY FOR THE LAS VEGAS GAME
(SINGLE-DECK)

THE DEALER'S UP-CARD

YOUR HAND	2	3	4	5	6	7	8	9	10	A
8	H	H	H	D	D	H	H	H	H	H
9	D	D	D	D	D	H	H	H	H	H
10	D	D	D	D	D	D	D	D	H	H
11	D	D	D	D	D	D	D	D	D	D
12	H	H	S	S	S	H	H	H	H	H
13	S	S	S	S	S	H	H	H	H	H
14	S	S	S	S	S	H	H	H	H	H
15	S	S	S	S	S	H	H	H	H	H
16	S	S	S	S	S	H	H	H	H	H
17	S	S	S	S	S	S	S	S	S	S
A,2	H	H	D	D	D	H	H	H	H	H
A,3	H	H	D	D	D	H	H	H	H	H
A,4	H	H	D	D	D	H	H	H	H	H
A,5	H	H	D	D	D	H	H	H	H	H
A,6	D	D	D	D	D	H	H	H	H	H
A,7	S	D	D	D	D	S	S	H	H	S
A,8	S	S	S	S	D	S	S	S	S	S
A,9	S	S	S	S	S	S	S	S	S	S
A,A	P	P	P	P	P	P	P	P	P	P
2,2	H	P	P	P	P	P	H	H	H	H
3,3	H	H	P	P	P	P	H	H	H	H
4,4	H	H	H	D	D	H	H	H	H	H
6,6	P	P	P	P	P	H	H	H	H	H
7,7	P	P	P	P	P	P	H	H	S	H
8,8	P	P	P	P	P	P	P	P	P	P
9,9	P	P	P	P	P	S	P	P	S	S
10,10	S	S	S	S	S	S	S	S	S	S

H = Hit. S = Stand. D = Double Down. P = Split.

CHART 10

BASIC STRATEGY FOR THE NORTHERN NEVADA GAME
(SINGLE-DECK)

THE DEALER'S UP-CARD

YOUR HAND	2	3	4	5	6	7	8	9	10	A
8	H	H	H	H	H	H	H	H	H	H
9	H	H	H	H	H	H	H	H	H	H
10	D	D	D	D	D	D	D	D	H	H
11	D	D	D	D	D	D	D	D	D	D
12	H	H	S	S	S	H	H	H	H	H
13	S	S	S	S	S	H	H	H	H	H
14	S	S	S	S	S	H	H	H	H	H
15	S	S	S	S	S	H	H	H	H	H
16	S	S	S	S	S	H	H	H	H	H
17	S	S	S	S	S	S	S	S	S	S
A,2	H	H	H	H	H	H	H	H	H	H
A,3	H	H	H	H	H	H	H	H	H	H
A,4	H	H	H	H	H	H	H	H	H	H
A,5	H	H	H	H	H	H	H	H	H	H
A,6	H	H	H	H	H	H	H	H	H	H
A,7	S	S	S	S	S	S	S	H	H	H
A,8	S	S	S	S	S	S	S	S	S	S
A,9	S	S	S	S	S	S	S	S	S	S
A,A	P	P	P	P	P	P	P	P	P	P
2,2	H	P	P	P	P	P	H	H	H	H
3,3	H	H	P	P	P	P	H	H	H	H
4,4	H	H	H	H	H	H	H	H	H	H
6,6	P	P	P	P	P	H	H	H	H	H
7,7	P	P	P	P	P	P	H	H	S	H
8,8	P	P	P	P	P	P	P	P	P	P
9,9	P	P	P	P	P	S	P	P	S	S
10,10	S	S	S	S	S	S	S	S	S	S

H = Hit. S = Stand. D = Double Down. P = Split.

you to play for the *short-run*. There are occasions when you should deviate from basic strategy either to protect your locked-up, short-run profits or to avoid risking them on hands with high bets. For example, the TAKEDOWN Strategy in Chapter 13 advises you to avoid doubling down under certain conditions associated with higher betting levels. Each of these deviations is explained clearly in the appropriate section of this book.

I recommend that you learn the basic strategy thoroughly so that you can play the hands automatically, without even thinking about them. Basic-strategy deviations occur infrequently, and *if you are uncertain about how to play any hand, basic strategy is always the correct play.* If you would like a wallet-sized card to carry with you on your casino visits, I will be happy to send you one for no charge. Just use the form in the back of this book to request it.

HOW TO LEARN BASIC STRATEGY

The drills and study procedures in this section are taken from my Basic-Strategy Home-Study Course.

General Memory Aids

Here are some tricks to help you memorize basic strategy for the shoe game.

For hitting and standing decisions, think in terms of low cards (2-6) and high cards (7-A) for the dealer's up-card. When the dealer shows a low card, you would never hit a breaking hand (12-16) with the exception of hitting 12 with a 2 or 3 showing. When the dealer shows a high card, always assume that his hole card is 10. Then it will be easy to remember that you must keep hitting your hand until you get hard 17 or better to beat the dealer's potential standing hand.

For doubling down on a hand totaling 9, remember that you double on 3-6; their sum is 9. For doubling on the soft hands, there is a pattern that will help you remember. For the lower soft hands (A,2 and A,3), you double down on 5 and 6 only. For the middle pair (A,4 and A,5), you add an up card and double down on 4, 5 and 6. And for the upper pair (A,6 and A,7) add an up card on the lower end: double down on 3,4,5 and 6.

Doubling-down rules for hands totaling 10 and 11 can be remembered as doubling on all up cards below the number: 10 is doubled on 2-9; 11 is doubled on 2-10.

Pair-split decisions can be remembered in groups. Twos, 3s and 7s are always split 2-7 (Atlantic City strategy). You can remember: 2s, 3s, 7s: 2-7. Nines (split 2-9 except 7) are easy to remember if you understand why the 7 is left out. A pair of 9s is 18 and will beat the dealer's potential 17. Sixes (split 2-6 for Atlantic City strategy) can be remembered as 6s to the 6 (2-6). For a pair of 4s, the memory aid is "4, 5, 6." Fours are split on 5 and 6 (Atlantic City strategy).

Finally, on pair splits, remember aces and 8s are always split; 5s and 10s are never split.

Basic-Strategy Rules for Hands Containing Three or More Cards

The following two rules apply for hard hands:

- Rule 1: Any multi-card hand that totals 11 or less is hit.
- Rule 2: Any multi-card hand that totals 12-21 is played using the hitting/standing strategy.

For multi-card soft hands, the following three rules apply:

- Rule 3: Always hit soft 17 or less. An example of a multi-card soft 17 is: A,2,4.
- Rule 4: Always stand on soft 19 or higher. An example of a multi-card soft 19 is A,5,3.
- Rule 5: For soft 18 stand on dealer up-cards 2-8; hit on dealer up-cards of 9, 10 and ace. An example of a multi-card soft 18 is A,3,4.

Note: should your soft hand turn hard, use Rules 1 and 2. For example: A,2,2 hit with an 8 becomes a hard 13 and you would use Rule 2.

Basic-Strategy Drills

1. Basic-Strategy Deck Drill

Using a single deck of cards, place one card face-up in front of you; this is the dealer's up-card. Now flip over two cards at a time. Each of these two-card pairs is your hand. Make a basic strategy decision for each hand against this same up card. Deal through the entire deck. Now shuffle the deck, change the up card and repeat the drill. Choose up cards that may be giving you problems in remembering.

Do not play out the dealer's hand in this drill.

An alternative procedure for this drill is to deal three cards at a time: an up card and your two-card hand. Play against a different up card for each two-card hand dealt.

This drill can be varied to work on various aspects of basic strategy. For example, to practice pair splits, set up a special training deck loaded with extra 2s, 3s, 4s, 5s, 6s and 7s. To practice doubling on 9, 10 and 11, load up a training deck with extra 4s, 5s and 6s.

To practice playing stiff hands, load up a training deck with extra 10-value cards and remove all neutral cards (7s, 8s and 9s). This drill is limited only by your imagination.

2. Basic-Strategy Soft-Hand Drill

To practice soft hands, give yourself a hand consisting of A,2 and play out the hand after giving the dealer an up card. After playing each hand, push the up card and the cards dealt to the A,2 aside and start over, dealing a new up card and playing from the A,2 as your first two cards.

3. Three-Card-Hand Drill

To practice multi-card hands, deal yourself a hand consisting of 3,2 and play out your hand after dealing the dealer his up card. You can change the up card for each hand or keep it constant until the shuffle. To practice playing stiff hands, start with a 10,3 instead of a 3,2.

4. Basic-Strategy Test

On a plain piece of $8\frac{1}{2} \times 11$ paper, write down the basic-strategy rules. Start with hitting and standing rules for hard and soft hands; then write down doubling-down rules for hard and soft hands; finally write down pair-split rules. Check your answers against the Basic Strategy tables in this book (see pp. 223–26).

5. Flash Cards

Flash cards are an excellent learning aid. You can make up your own by purchasing some light cardboard stock at your local stationery store. Cut the stock into one- or two-inch squares. Write down each hand on one side and the correct basic-strategy play for that hand on the reverse. Use the flash cards to test yourself on each hand. For instance, suppose your flash card shows a 13 as the hand to be played. Recite the correct play for 13 before turning the flash card over to check yourself: stand on 2-6; hit on 7 or higher.

Use the enclosed information Request Card if you would like to order a set of flash cards through my office.

21

Glossary of Terms

BACK-COUNTING A player standing in back of the table, behind the other players, keeping a count and waiting for the count to rise to the level where he or she has a mathematical advantage over the dealer, at which point he or she enters the game.

BANKROLL All the money a player sets aside for risking at blackjack. The bankroll is divided into betting units according to the risk a player wishes to take.

BLACKJACK A card game played between a dealer and one to seven players. Cards are dealt in succession with each player receiving two cards. One of the dealer's two cards is exposed. The value of each hand is determined by adding the values of the two cards. Face cards count 10 and all other cards count their face value (i.e., 5 counts as 5) except ace, which counts as either 1 or 11, at the player's option. The object of the game is to beat the dealer while not going over 21 (breaking). Following the initial deal of two cards, each player, in turn, is permitted to draw as many cards as he or she wishes. If a player breaks (goes over 21), he immediately loses his bet. After all the players have drawn cards, the dealer turns over his unexposed card and draws cards as long as he has 16 or less. If the dealer's hand totals 17 or more, he cannot draw another card.

Blackjack also refers to a "natural" 21: the combination of an ace and a 10 or face card, dealt on the first two cards. The player is immediately paid one and one half his or her bet unless the dealer also has a blackjack.

BET   The amount of money wagered by a player against the dealer within betting limits established by the house. A table accepting $1 minimum bets may have a betting maximum of $300; a table with $5 minimum bets may have a betting maximum of $3000. Signs are usually posted to inform players of betting minimums and maximums for each table.

BIAS   Sometimes the result of the non-random shuffle employed by all casino dealers. In general, a game in which the dealer is beating the majority of the players is considered a dealer-biased game; a game in which 50% or more of the players are defeating the dealer is considered a player-biased game.

BREAK (BUST)   Exceed 21 points. If a player breaks, he immediately turns over his cards, and the dealer takes his bet. If the dealer breaks, he or she immediately pays all of the players who did not bust previously.

BURN CARD   After the deck or decks are shuffled and cut, one card is placed at the bottom of the pack or in the discard tray. This is called burning a card. A few casinos burn more than one card, but this is not a common practice.

BUY-IN   The amount of money the player exchanges for chips when he or she enters the game.

CHIP (CHECK)   A token used in lieu of money to make the bets. A $5 chip is worth $5. Chips are color-coded and marked by the issuing casino.

COUNTER   A player who counts cards.

A player who uses a counting system to keep track of the types of cards played in order to determine whether the deck or shoe is mathematically favorable or unfavorable.

CUT   The process of splitting the deck or decks after the dealer has completed the shuffling process.

CUT CARD   A solid-colored card, the same size as a playing card, used by a player to indicate a desired cut to the dealer. After the cut card is inserted into the deck or decks by the player, the cards are then cut at that location by the dealer.

DEALER   A casino employee who deals the game of blackjack. The dealer plays according to a predetermined set of rules. He must hit all his hands that total 16 or less. He may or may not hit a soft

17, depending on the casino. He plays against each player in succession and settles all bets at the end of a round of play.

DOUBLE DOWN (DOUBLE)   The doubling of a bet on the first two cards; in this case, the player is dealt only one more card. Doubling down is advantageous if the player's hand totals 10 or 11, for example, because a 10 would give him a 20 or 21.

FLAT BET   A bet of the same amount on each hand.

FLASHER   A dealer, who, when peeking at the hole card, inadvertently "flashes" its value to the first-base player—the player sitting to the dealer's immediate left.

FRONT LOADING   A player who sits at the table in such a way, usually slumped way down in the chair, to make possible the determination of the dealer's hole card. Front loading refers to the process, not the player.

GAME-CONTROL METHODS   Procedures in which the casino attempts to disrupt a game in which an excessive amount of money is being won by players. Such procedures may include simply changing the cards or introducing stripping, which, by the dealer's removal of small clumps from the bottom, top or middle of the pick, reverses the order of the cards during the shuffling process. Another common method is the introduction of the unbalanced shuffle, in which the dealer makes unequal picks for the purpose of inhibiting distribution. These game-control methods do not represent forms of cheating and may not necessarily have an impact on the game.

HARD HAND   Any hand that totals 12 or more without an ace (or with an ace valued as 1).

For example, a player drawing an ace to a two-card total of 16 would have a hard hand of 17.

HIT   The player's decision to take another card. He may do this as long as he does not have 21. Most players, however, never hit a hand 17 or higher.

HOLE CARD   The unexposed card in the dealer's two-card hand; it is not shown until all of the player's hands have been played.

INSURANCE   A bet allowed when the dealer shows an ace. The player is allowed to bet half his or her original bet that the dealer has a 10 underneath, and thus a blackjack. If the dealer does have a blackjack, the insurance bet is paid at 2 to 1. The player loses his original bet unless he has a blackjack, in which case his original bet is pushed. If the dealer does not have a blackjack, the insurance is lost, and the play continues. The insurance bet is paid whenever the dealer checks the hole card and determines whether or not he has the blackjack.

MARKER   A casino check or draft used by the player to draw chips against credit or money on deposit with the casino.

PAT HAND   A hand, usually 17 or above, to which no further cards are drawn.

PIT BOSS   A casino employee who supervises a number of blackjack dealers and floor personnel. "Pit boss" is sometimes inaccurately used to describe a floor person or general supervisor. Pit bosses are in charge of designated blackjack tables and consider requests for complimentary services from players, monitor inexperienced dealers, watch for cheating, referee floor disputes and handle paperwork for scheduling employees. Floor personnel or general supervisors also monitor dealers and games while acting as hosts and hostesses to the players, particularly credit players.

POINT COUNT   The evaluation of odds via a tally of assigned points. A number is assigned to each card according to the value of that card toward making up a winning hand for the player. For example, each 2,3,4,5 or 6 counts as $+1$; each 7,8, or 9 counts as 0; each 10, J, Q, K or ace counts as -1. The point count is computed at the end of each hand by adding the counts for each card played in that hand to the point count at the end of the previous hand. For example, if 6, 4, 10, ace, 8, and 3 are dealt off the top of a fresh deck, the point count is $+1$. This is computed as follows:

$$6 = +1; 4 = +1; 10 = -1; A = -1; 8 = 0; 3 = +1$$
$$+1+1-1-1+0+1 = +1$$

PLAYER'S ADVANTAGE (ODDS, EXPECTATION)   The percent of all money wagered that a player can expect to win in the long run. This number is computed by statistical methods and depends on the particular system the player employs. If a player enjoys a 2% advantage, he or she will win, in the long run, 2% of the total amount of money bet. If a player has a 0% expectation, he will break even over a period of time. If his expectation is -10%, he will eventually lose ten cents out of each dollar bet.

PUSH   A tie between a player and the dealer; no money changes hands.

RANK   The defined value of each card. The 9 of clubs has a rank of 9. The queen of spades has a rank of 10.

RANK COUNT   The number of a particular rank that has been played and counted. Refers to those systems in which a particular rank, such as 10s, aces, or 5s, are counted. Raising one's bet on a deficiency of 5s is a rank-count system.

RUNNING COUNT   The point count updated as each card is played or dealt by the dealer instead of at the end of the round.

SCOUT (VERB)   To look for a good game.

SESSION   Amount of time devoted to play without interruption. A player might play a two-hour session.

SHUFFLE   At a predetermined spot in the deck or shoe, the dealer stops the game and mixes the cards according to a procedure usually prescribed by casino management.

SHUFFLE-TRACKING   A method of keeping track of specific cards through the shuffling procedure.

SPLIT   A situation in which the player has two like cards (a pair; e.g., 6, 6). He may play the cards as two separate hands, making another bet exactly equal to the amount of his original bet.

SOFT HAND   Any hand containing an ace that totals 21 or less with the ace valued as 11.

STAND (STICK)   The player's decision not to take any additional cards.

STIFF   Any hand between 12 and 16, inclusive, where the player or dealer has a chance of breaking.

STOP-LOSS   An amount of money which, if lost, signals the end of play at this table or for this session.

STOP-WIN   The achievement of a winning goal might trigger an end to play for this session. A player usually establishes this stop-win before the session starts.

SYSTEM (STRATEGY)   The method of play. The basic strategy is an optimized method that involves rules for taking insurance, surrendering, splitting, doubling down, hitting, or standing. Other systems or strategies may involve card counting for determining the player's advantage or disadvantage and possible variations from basic strategy for the play of certain hands.

SURRENDER   When the house rules permit, a decision made by a player to throw in the first two cards and surrender half the wager. If a player is allowed to make this play before the dealer turns over the hole card, it is called "early surrender." "Late surrender" enables a player to make the same play only after it has been determined that the dealer does not have a blackjack.

TARGET   TARGET stands for *Ta*ble *R*esearch, *G*rading & *E*valuation *T*echnique. It is a proprietary strategy marketed by Jerry Patterson that involves using 18 factors to select player-biased or dealer-breaking games. TARGET 21 is a process for finding winning tables, a method for exploiting these tables to maximize profits and a tactic for departing the tables when the bias turns to favor the dealer.

TEAM   A group of players who combine their bankrolls, playing time and skills for the purpose of winning more money than if they were playing alone. Also refers to two or more players who cooperate to find more playable tables in a casino.

TELL   A "tell" is a subconscious dealer body-mannerism which the experienced player can read to determine the value of the hole card.

TODAY'S PLAYER   A blackjack player who recognizes that a casino-played game of blackjack is different than a computer-played game of blackjack and who recognizes the shortcomings of card-counting strategies in blackjack as it is played today. Also a player who is trained to play for the short-term, an evening or weekend, as opposed to the long-term—hundreds of hours of play.

TOKE   A tip or a wager placed for the dealer.

TRADITIONAL PLAYER   A player who plays card-counting strategies for the long-term. Sometimes disparagingly referred to as a player who does not understand the realities of today's game.

TRUE COUNT   Running count adjusted to reflect the number of decks or cards remaining to be played. Also called "count per deck."

UNIT   Dollar amount wagered as basic bet. For example, a player might divide a $1000 bankroll into 100 betting units of $10 each.

WASH   To mix up new decks of cards at the beginning of the day or shift. After checking new cards for possible markings, the dealer lays them on the table and swirls them in a "washing" motion prior to executing the shuffle. Cards are usually clumped to favor the dealer after the wash, and the astute player waits at least two hours after the wash before entering any shoe game.

PART SIX

Products and Services Available to the Interested Reader

22

Products and Services Offered by Jerry Patterson

The goal of this book is to teach you how to beat the casinos, to take the money off the blackjack tables in any casinos in the world. To this end, and within proprietary restrictions, I believe I have given you, the reader, more winning tools, tactics, strategies and methods than any book ever published on blackjack.

As you now know from reading this book, I am both a developer of, and instructor in, winning blackjack methods. If you are interested in higher-level instruction, instruction from where this book leaves off, I invite you to contact me. The systems and methods in this book teach you to exploit biased games when you find yourself in one. But my proprietary TARGET 21 Method teaches you *how to find a winning table.* I do not market this method to the gaming public. I would rather have you, an educated reader and player, come to me and inquire. Based on the information you receive, if you feel you can extend your knowledge and increase your winnings, I will be happy to work with you.

Read on, then, and inquire if your interest is piqued. This section describes home-study courses and classes that I have developed for those interested in acquiring additional knowledge for beating the casinos.

Although an active professional gambler spending much of my time at the blackjack tables and managing my investments in the stock and commodity futures and options markets, I am committed to serving the needs of beginning, intermediate and experienced gamblers. This is accomplished by offering the products and services described in this chapter.

THE TARGET 21 INSTRUCTIONAL PROGRAM

TARGET 21, which stands for *Ta*ble, *R*esearch, *G*rading & *E*valuation *T*echnique, is a method for finding winning tables. We call these tables *player-biased tables* or *dealer-breaking tables*. They result from biases caused by the non-random shuffle.

Many players, after reading my books, are curious about the method and call me with questions. Here are some typical ones:

Why Teach TARGET 21? Why Not Just Keep It for Yourself?

I do. I'm a professional player dividing my time between Atlantic City and Nevada. I'm also probably the only blackjack teacher who oftentimes plays right alongside his students. That's why we offer TARGET 21 weekend classes in casino cities. The casinos themselves are the best teaching laboratory there is.

But I have always been an entrepreneur, looking for products that fill a need and then forming businesses to market them. I enjoy teaching and I enjoy showing gamblers how to win. Nancy and I have operated *The Blackjack Clinic and School of Gambling* since 1977; we make a fair profit, but to be in business this long, we must be doing something right.

Is TARGET 21 Just for Experienced Players or Professional Players?

No. the 18 factors that point to winning tables are easily learned. Many successful TARGET 21 players visit the casinos just once a month; some only play once or twice a year.

If you learn to play with an edge over the house, you can win. Without training, you have a very good chance of losing on most of your trips. Remember that playing with basic strategy is still a losing game. *Disciplined TARGET 21 players win 6 to 7 trips out of 10.*

What Do the Casinos Do to Stop TARGET 21 Players From Winning?

If you are a card counter, the casinos can tell if they have someone watching your betting pattern. The betting pattern of a card counter is easily detectable. But with TARGET 21, there is no way to detect you. You look like an ordinary gambler, since you raise your bet when winning and lower it or walk away when losing. Granted you win more often; but to a pit boss you look like a gambler, so they don't worry.

When the dealer is running cold, the casinos could bring in new decks of cards, but this is very time consuming. It aggravates the players and costs the casinos money. They lose money by not dealing during the down time required to remove the cards from boxes, examine them for marks, "wash" the cards and perform the new shuffle.

If I Am Already a Card Counter, How Would TARGET 21 Help My Game?

You use TARGET 21 to select the tables with a bias in your favor and, after table entry, you start to count. In many cases the count works better at these tables (you do have to verify this however, by analyzing a TARGET 21 factor called "Integrity") and you will not have the downswings prevalent in many dealer-biased games.

In many dealer-biased games the count does not work for reasons discussed in this book. For example, the count goes up, but the high cards do not come out as predicted, or they come out in the disadvantageous like-card clumps. The TARGET 21 Course teaches you how to avoid these games.

When Counting, Do I Have to Memorize Cards When I Play? Will It Take the Fun Out of the Game?

No. You don't have to memorize cards at all. First of all, you don't have to count when you use TARGET 21. And, if you do count, all you have to remember is just one number, because each card you see is either added to or subtracted from that running-count number.

Playing with TARGET 21 is fun because you don't have to concentrate if you are not counting. You will enjoy talking to the other players; players at your tables will be more talkative because they are at winning tables that you have selected.

Experiment: On your next trip to the casino, walk around and notice how few people at the blackjack tables look like they are having a good time. You won't see many because most tables are losing tables; and losing is no fun.

How Difficult Is It to Learn?

It is not difficult. The minimum time required is eight to nine hours. It takes that long to go through the audio and video tapes. TARGET 21 is very logical, which makes it easy to learn and remember. After listening to the audio tapes, watching the video tape and reading over the course materials, you will know most of the TARGET 21 factors.

How Many TARGET 21 Factors Are There?

Eighteen. If you see 6 or more, you have a high probability of a winning table. In the TARGET 21 Home-Study Course, we teach you how to recognize these factors and evaluate them for a table-entry decision. In the early '80s, when we first started using and teaching TARGET 21, there were just 7 factors. Research has continued over the years and confirmed the existence of 18, 4 of which we call Superfactors because of their extremely strong correlation to winning tables.

When Will TARGET 21 Be Published in One of Your Books?

Probably never. The method is proprietary and is just too valuable. TARGET is not a system I ever advertise. The only players who acquire the method are ones who take the time to contact me after reading this or another of my books.

Could I Play Blackjack as a Way of Generating Extra Income?

This is the goal of many of our users. We know they succeed because they come to Update Sessions and we survey them periodically. Others use TARGET 21 to build a large bankroll so they can enjoy the thrill of betting "green" ($25 chips) or "black" ($100 chips). And still others use their blackjack winnings to finance their trips and vacations to exotic locations.

Can You Describe the Course?

TARGET 21 is offered both as a Home-Study Course and a Weekend Class Experience in Atlantic City, Las Vegas or Reno/Tahoe.

The TARGET 21 Home-Study Course includes **audio and video tape instruction, training manuals and telephone consultation.** It features in-casino instruction with a small group of students conducted by me or one of my instructors (this is done in such a way that the pit bosses do not know what we are doing). In addition, TARGET 21 Update Seminars are offered periodically. TARGET 21 is a unique instructional program and your inquiries are invited. Please call my office **toll free** for a **free 12-page brochure** or use the coupon at the back of this chapter to request one. An outline of the course follows.

TARGET 21 COURSE OUTLINE

Lesson 1: Understanding TARGET 21 and Why You Win

— How to Select a Moneymaking Table
— How One TARGET 21 Superfactor Can Almost Guarantee Your Profits

— When to Leave the Table With Profits in Hand

— How and Why TARGET 21 Solves the Problems Associated with Card Counting

— How to Use TARGET 21 to Pick Tables Where the Count Really Works

— Definitions of Bias and Non-random Shuffles and How They Work to Your Advantage

— Why the "Wash" Makes Certain Games Off-Limits

— Understanding the Different Types of Shuffles and How They Work to Your Advantage or Disadvantage

— Special Drills for TARGET 21 Casino Practice

Lesson 2: Exploiting TARGET 21's Profit Potential

— Questions and Answers From a Live TARGET 21 Classroom Session

— How to Increase Your Profits by Using a Disciplined Documentation Method

— Money Management: Flat Betting (Betting the Same Amount) and When to Use It

— Money Management: When to Bet and When Not to Bet With the Count

— Money Management: Special Techniques for Recreational Gamblers, High Rollers and Junket Players

— Tips for Creating the "Home-Run Tables" Where the Dealer Breaks Hand After Hand

— How to "Tune" Your Play to Exploit the Special Advantages in the Atlantic City Game

— Nuances for the Variety of Games in Nevada

— "Action TARGET": Amazing Moneymaking Opportunities for Nevada's Single-Deck Games

— When and How to Avoid Losing by Standing on Stiff Hands

— How to Evaluate a Casino for TARGET 21 Play

Lesson 3: Casino Session (two Hours in the Casino With Jerry and a Small Group)

— How the Casino Session Works

— Instructor Selects TARGET 21 Tables for Review and Comment

— Students Practice Scouting and Table Selection with Instructor Feedback (away from the casino floor)

— Instructor Monitors Table Departure

TARGET 21 course materials include (1) six hours of audio-cassette tapes, (2) two hours of videotape, (3) a comprehensive training manual, (4) a portfolio of expanded TARGET course materials and follow-up support: access to TARGET hotline; telephone consultation with Jerry Patterson; and TARGET 21 Update Seminars in Atlantic City, Las Vegas and Reno/Tahoe—all at no additional cost—ever.

Call TOLL FREE 1-800-257-7130 and ask for FREE 12-page brochure which describes the TARGET Method. Or send us the Information Request Coupon at the back of this chapter.

Please note that if you decide to order this unique instructional program, you take absolutely no risk because you are protected by an unconditional and legally binding guarantee.

THE CASINO GAMBLERS' NETWORK™

Luxury and power permeate the casino environment. Excitement flows with each toss of the dice, spin of the wheel, pull of the handle and deal of the cards. The atmosphere is charged with expectation. Every gambler expects to win and be the "lucky one" to take home a piece of the casino's bankroll.

Have you ever experienced the joy of winning? The sheer adrenaline high that comes with grabbing two or three times your pocket bankroll and going home with this money?

This is what **The Casino Gamblers' Network**™ is all about; the goal is to teach you how to win, how to increase your winning sessions and decrease your losing sessions and take the money home; whether its off the blackjack tables, at craps, or even roulette or baccarat.

The Casino Gamblers' Network tm is many things, but information dissemination and exchange are paramount.

The components of the Network are: Gamblers' Clinics, a Gamblers' Newsletter, a Gamblers' Hotline, Certified Systems and Methods, Gambling Tours and Adventures, and many other benefits.

Most gamblers need education on how to play the games, how to make the best bets and avoid the worst bets and how to gamble within the constraints of their bankroll. This need is satisfied by *Gamblers' Clinics* conducted periodically in Atlantic City, Las Vegas and Reno. Information on systems that work and about casinos that offer the best playing conditions is exchanged.

There are literally hundreds of systems and methods that have been devised to "beat the gambling games" or, more realistically, to make the gamblers' money last as long as possible. The uneducated gambler has no way of evaluating these systems and deciding which, if any, meets his or her needs. **The Casino Gamblers Network** tm evaluates systems, subjects them to the scrutiny of a **System Certification Board,** publishes the results in the *Gamblers' Newsletter* and, if appropriate, publishes the system itself. The gambler is given a series of factors about each system that can be used to determine whether or not the system meets his or her needs.

The gambler's chances of winning at blackjack, craps, roulette and even the slot and videopoker machines vary greatly among the casinos. The gambler needs information about the odds his or her favourite casino offers and about which casinos offer the best odds in the gambling games. **The Casino Gamblers' Network** tm satisfies this information need by making available to its members a *Gamblers' Hotline.* For example, the *Gamblers' Hotline* offers information about the best blackjack rules, where to find single-zero roulette tables, where to find the best videopoker rules and which casinos offer the highest jackpots on their videopoker machines. **The hotline is updated as conditions change, and the gambler calls before any casino trip to find out those casinos with the best conditions.**

Many gamblers would like to connect with other gamblers with common interests for visits to the casino, practice sessions and so forth. The Network makes this possible through a *Gamblers' Newsletter* and also through the *Gamblers' Clinics.* The newsletter also publishes a variety of information about the gambling games, including certified systems, book and system reviews and other news of interest.

The Casino Gamblers' Network ^{tm} offers a myriad of other benefits. For example, gamblers love to travel. And they enjoy traveling with other gamblers. The Network offers *Gambling Tours and Adventures*— organized tours with instruction to such destinations as Reno/Tahoe, Las Vegas and Atlantic City.

Please use the form in the back of this book to request detailed information. Or call the toll-free number. Ask about the low membership rates.

COMPUTER-ASSISTED BLACKJACK TUTOR

Custom-designed for use with most personal computers, the Computer-Assisted Blackjack Tutor will enable a player with just elementary knowledge of basic strategy, card counting and money management to become a highly skilled card counter. The program includes the High-Low Card-Counting System—easiest to learn, easiest to play, used by more players than any other system and rivaling the most advanced counting method for efficiency. The player may set parameters to describe the type of blackjack game he or she wishes to play: number of decks, number of players, cut-card placement, money-management strategy and many others. You are invited to request a free brochure. Use the Information Request Coupon.

OTHER PRODUCTS AND SERVICES AVAILABLE FROM JERRY PATTERSON

Please feel free to inquire about the other products and services I offer:

1. Sports Betting Services (Football, Basketball and Baseball)
2. Professional Level, Winning Craps Method
3. Financial Investment Program (Stock Options, Low-priced Stocks, Commodity Futures, Long-term Investment Strategies)
4. Recommendations for instructors of thoroughbred and Standard-bred handicapping

23

Products and Services Recommended by Jerry Patterson

PLAYERS CLUB INTERNATIONAL

If you visit a casino once a year or more often, you can't afford to be without the benefits of The Players Club. The club has been organized to bring all of the casino benefits—heretofore available to high rollers and players with large credit lines—to occasional and recreational gamblers and weekend players.

Here's what you receive when you join:

Guaranteed Savings: a minimum of 25 to 60% off your hotel room rate. Twenty-five percent off meals and drinks even at the gourmet restaurants. Twenty-five percent off shows for up to four people.

VIP Privileges: Pass by the show lines for immediate VIP entrance; special hotel check-in area that avoids lines; invitations to casino parties and sporting events.

Monthly Hot Sheet: Features special room rates and prices at various member casinos; information on cruises, contests and other good deals.

Hotel and Travel Reservations: One call to Players Club and they will take care of all your casino travel needs; they will also get you the lowest possible air fares with cancellation privileges.

Car Rentals: Discounts at major car-rental agencies.

Accommodations are at first-class casino/hotels in Nevada, Atlantic City and other international locations. They also have arrangements with cruise ships and can handle all your needs in this area as well.

Please return the information request form and we will send you a package of information on The Players Club.

THE PLAYER—AMERICA'S GAMING GUIDE

The annual subscription of only $20 is a real bargain because when you subscribe, your fee is returned many times over with free coins, tokens, show tickets and other benefits available through certain casinos.

The major reason I like this gambling newsmagazine and am recommending it to you is that it covers the broad spectrum of gambling, including winning tactics and money-management ideas on all the table games, slots, poker, sports betting and horserace handicapping. It also features interviews with the top entertainers appearing in casino locations with one of the best interviewers in the business.

So now, whether you are new to the gambling scene or already a seasoned pro, there's an information-packed publication that gets you on the inside track of all the casino and entertainment action in Atlantic City, Nevada and the Caribbean.

Please return the Information Request Form and we will send you a package of information on *The Player.*

GAMBLER'S BOOK CLUB AND OTHER GAMBLING BOOKSTORES

We have already reviewed the Gambler's Book Club in Chapter 10 as the source of all of your gambling information needs, including books and newsletters that are difficult to find elsewhere. The Gambler's Book Club is located at 630 S. 11th Street, Las Vegas, Nevada.

This is right off Charleston Blvd. and just five minutes from the Las Vegas Strip.

There are other gambling bookstores that you should be aware of that offer many of the same products and services as the original Gambler's Book Club. These are:

Gambler's World: 3914 NW Grand Ave., Phoenix, AZ 85019
Gambler's Book Store: 135 N Sierra St., Reno, NV
Gambler's General Store: 800 S Main, Las Vegas, NV 89101
Atlantic City News Agency: 101 S Illinois, Atlantic City, NJ

Please tear out and send this form or a copy to: Jerry
Patterson; P.O. Box 3040; Carson City, NV 89702.

INFORMATION REQUEST FORM

For faster service call **TOLL FREE: 1-800-257-7130.**

Dear Jerry,

I am interested in the following:

[ ] Blackjack/TARGET 21 Method. Please send me a 12-page
brochure on this Home-Study Course with Audio and Video tapes.

[ ] Send me information on your weekend classes held in casino
cities and which use the casinos as a learning laboratory.

[ ] Please send me information on your **Casino Gamblers'
Network** tm which explains the Network services: clinics, newsletters,
systems and methods exchange, hotline, how to connect with other
gamblers and gambling tours and adventures.

[ ] Please send me a free wallet-sized basic strategy card for [ ]
Atlantic City; [ ] Las Vegas Strip; [ ] Las Vegas Downtown; [ ] Reno and
northern Nevada

[ ] Please send me a set of basic-strategy flash cards for the casino
location checked above. Enclosed is $3 to cover postage and handling.

[ ] Please send information on your Blackjack Tutor for my personal
computer. Computer Type: _____

[ ] Please send me information on your Sports Betting Service:
{ } Football { } Basketball { } Baseball

[ ]Please send me information on your Professional Level, Winning
Craps Method

[ ] Please send me information on your Financial Success Program
which explains the advantage of investing in stock options and
low-priced stocks.

[ ] *Players Club* (Casino Travel and VIP Club). Please send me
information package with special offer.

[ ] *The Player* (Gambling Newsmagazine). Please send me
information package with special offer.

[ ] Please send me names of instructors and professional horse
players whom I can contact for instruction

Name: _____

Address: _____

City/State/Zip: _____

Phone: _____